WORTH K

'The real life stories in this
women who have each learnt to near God's song
over them. Any woman reading them will be inspired to
hear that song for themselves and to live more in line with
God's design for them.'

Sila Lee

'I read the book in one afternoon - a great resource and a
good read with some very moving real-life stories, and
loads of down-to-earth lived-out wisdom.'

Debby Wright

'This book is a joy to read. It's packed with testimonies and
teaching that will inspire, instruct and uplift you. If
you're a woman with a heart to follow God, buy this book!'

Beth Redman

WORTH KNOWING

Wisdom for Women

Edited and compiled by
ALI HERBERT

Including chapters by
Mary Pytches, Fiona Castle, Amy Orr-Ewing,
Jo Saxton, Michele Guinness and
Diane-Louise Jordan

survivor

Unless otherwise indicated, biblical quotations are from
the New International Version © 1973, 1978, 1984
by the International Bible Society.

ISBN 978-1-84291-325-3

Survivor is an imprint of
KINGSWAY COMMUNICATIONS LTD
Lottbridge Drove, Eastbourne BN23 6NT, England.
Email: books@kingsway.co.uk

Printed in the USA

Contents

Acknowledgements 7

Biographies 8

Introduction – **Ali Herbert** 13

1 Who Am I Really? – **Mary Pytches** 17

2 The Names God Speaks Over Us – **Ali MacInnes** 27

God at Work: Clare's Story 39

3 Do You Fancy a Coffee Sometime? – **Jo Saxton
and Sally Breen** 43

4 Woman in the Workplace – **Michele Guinness** 59

God at Work: Irene's Story 71

5 Travelling in Excess – **Diane-Louise Jordan** 77

6 Living Without Regrets – **Fiona Castle** 85

God at Work: Debs' Story 93

7 Can't Stop That Lovin' Feeling – **Annie Kirke and Minu Westlake** 99

8 Women of Worship – **Vicky Beeching** 115

God at Work: Jean's Story 127

9 Life in a Postmodern World – **Amy Orr-Ewing** 133

10 Designed by God – **Rachel Hughes** 145

God at Work: Cheryll's Story 157

11 Keep Smiling! Dealing with Crises in Our Lives – **Elke Werner** 163

12 Just Finish It, Baby – **Ali Herbert** 171

Acknowledgements

I'd like to thank Les Moir and Richard Herkes at Kingsway and Survivor; John & Jenny Peters and Barry & Mary Kissell for their inspiring leadership and prophetic insight; my mum and dad – Jill & Henry Rattle – for their spiritual (and grammatical) wisdom; Anna Hayward and Maggie Sandilands for reading and commenting on the manuscript; Nick my husband for his endless supply of enthusiasm and encouragement, and Gracie our daughter for sleeping so I could work on the manuscript! And thank you too to all the women who have been involved in Girlzone events at St Mary's, Bryanston Square for helping me learn to lead and for worshipping God with all your hearts and being hungry for more.

Biographies

Vicky Beeching

Vicky is a worship leader and songwriter who has worked within the Vineyard Movement and Soul Survivor Ministries. She currently lives in the United States, signed to record label EMI. A graduate of Oxford University, with an MA in Theology, she also loves to teach and write on biblical matters.

Sally Breen

Sally has been married for 25 years to Mike and has three nearly grown-up children. She has worked alongside her husband in church leadership and in mentoring young adults for about 20 years. She loves interior design, clothes, the television drama 24 and her new iPod, as well as – of course – Mike, Beccy, Libby and Sam who make her laugh, often at herself. Sally lives in Phoenix, Arizona.

Fiona Castle

Fiona was born in 1940 in the Wirral. At the age of nine she went to Elmhurst Ballet School and went on to work in the theatre. She was introduced to Roy Castle, the entertainer, by a mutual friend, Eric Morecambe. Roy and Fiona married in 1963 and had four children. They had been married for 31 years when Roy died of cancer in 1994. Since then Fiona has written ten books and has had a regular daily slot on London's Premier Radio for five years. She speaks at a variety of events and is patron of a number of charities. She ran the London Marathon for the first time in 2001 and again in 2005, probably for the final time!

Michele Guinness

Brought up in a practising Jewish family and converted to Christianity as a teenager, Michele Guinness was until recently Head of Communications for the Cumbria and Lancashire Strategic Health Authority, and is now a communications consultant and trainer. She has written eight books, including *Child of the Covenant*, her autobiography, and *Woman, the Full Story*. She is married to Peter, an Anglican clergyman, and they have two grown-up children.

Ali Herbert

After finishing an MA in Text and Performance at RADA and King's College, London, Ali worked as an actor and musician for several years before having a baby in 2004. She is now enjoying being a full-time mum, playing keyboards now and again in the band Pastiche and songwriting in any spare time! Ali heads up the Girlzone women's ministry and is on the PCC of St Mary's in central London. She is married to Nick and they have a daughter called Gracie.

Rachel Hughes

Rachel lives in London with her husband Tim, and works as the Video Production Manager at Holy Trinity, Brompton. Rachel's passion is to see young women 'throw off everything that hinders' and step wholeheartedly into the potential that God has for them.

Diane-Louise Jordan

Diane's extensive television work on programmes such as *Songs of Praise* and *Blue Peter* earned her the description 'presenter across boundaries'. As a mother, author, committed Christian and businesswoman, Diane is also invited to speak at corporate and Christian conferences, and high-profile charity events throughout the country.

Annie Kirke

Annie is 31 and lives in London. She studied French and Spanish at Cardiff University and has a Masters in International Relations. Annie worked in South Africa for two and a half years with Soul Survivor and returned to the UK in 2001, where she has been working for Tearfund ever since. She has been involved in various ministries at St Mary's, Bryanston Square for four years. She loves skiing, running and going out with friends.

Ali MacInnes

Ali works with Soul Survivor, a youth ministry which aims to reach young people with the good news of Jesus and to see them released and equipped to follow him. As well as heading up Soul Sista, the girls-only wing of Soul

Survivor, she also spends part of her time travelling to other countries around the world being part of what Soul Survivor is doing there. She is passionate about seeing God's people grow in freedom as they understand more about God and who he created them to be.

Amy Orr-Ewing

Amy is Training Director of The Zacharias Trust. She gained a first-class degree in Theology at Christ Church, Oxford, and a Masters in Theology at King's College, London. Amy speaks at many universities, churches and conferences. She has co-authored (with her husband) *Holy Warriors: A Fresh Look at the Face of Extreme Islam* and has contributed to the book *God and the Generations*. Her new book *Why Trust the Bible?* was shortlisted for the 2006 UK Christian Book Awards. She is married to Frog (Francis), a vicar in the Church of England, and they live in London with their twin boys.

Mary Pytches

Mary, her husband David and their four daughters spent 17 years in Chile as missionaries before coming back to St Andrew's, Chorleywood, from where the New Wine conferences were birthed. Mary has written a number of books and, though retired, still enjoys speaking and travelling.

Jo Saxton

Jo loves being married to her husband Chris and mother to their daughter Tia. In her spare time (?) she serves in church leadership, disciples young adult women and writes stuff! Jo believes a woman can never have too many shoes, handbags or caramel macchiatos. Jo lives in Phoenix, Arizona.

Elke Werner

Elke was born in Duisburg, Germany, in 1956. She lives with her husband Roland in Marburg, a quaint medieval university town in the geographical centre of Germany. Together they founded and lead Christus-Treff, an ecumenical, evangelical community with centres in Marburg, Berlin and Jerusalem. Elke is a trained teacher and author of many books. She travels widely to speak at women's conferences internationally. Elke serves as Senior Associate for Women in the International Lausanne Movement for World Evangelisation.

Minu Westlake

Minu currently works as Director of Communications at the Church Urban Fund. Over the years she has moved between the commercial and voluntary sectors, working in the areas of fundraising and communications. She has also worked full time for churches and mission agencies. She has been involved in planting and developing two youth congregations that are now 'grown-up' churches. Minu is married to David and has a young daughter called Ellie.

Introduction

Ali Herbert

In 2002 I heard Mary Pytches giving a talk at a New Wine Christian conference. I felt God telling me to set up some women's conferences back in my home church of St Mary's in London. To be honest, I laughed because I have never really been the sort of person who was interested in going to 'women's' events, let alone running them. I suppose there was a streak in me thinking that we shouldn't need separate 'gender' meetings, or that women's stuff would be too touchy-feely and oversentimental – things I thought I was way too cool for. Well, as you can imagine, God had a few things to say to me on that subject!

As I wouldn't willingly have dreamt up the idea myself, I decided it probably was God asking me to do it. So I went home, was given the blessing of our church leaders, thought about the women I would like to speak and who would lead worship, and simply asked them. They all said 'yes'. That was the start of the Girlzone events at our church, bringing together lots of women primarily in their 20s and 30s. It has been great fun and while there has been plenty of emotional stuff coming up, we've loved meeting together as women, really worshipped God, been challenged and found out more about ourselves in the process. I hadn't realised how powerful it could be to meet as a large group of women, nor the different dynamic and freedom it would offer not having guys around.

We've been blessed at our Girlzone events to have some great speakers and it seemed a little unfair to keep their 'words of wisdom for women in the world' to ourselves! And so the idea for this compilation was born.

In this book you will find essays and articles on a variety of topics – from relationships to worship to work – but I hope all of them will be affirming, challenging and practically helpful. They are by women, for women – but the wisdom in them is for everybody, so feel free to pass this book on to your boyfriends, husbands and male friends. They might just learn something too.

Life stories are a powerful testimony to God's grace and his interest in us, so there are sections of the book called 'God at Work'. It's good to hear of God's ongoing process of rescuing, healing and encouraging us.

God is interested in people. He is interested in *you*. As you listen to the different voices talking about different topics in this book, I hope that this message will come across loud and clear. It's not always easy being a Christian woman, but be encouraged: we're in this together! Unique as each of us is, and free to express ourselves in different ways, we can enjoy being daughters of the same Heavenly Father and together celebrate the everyday challenge of becoming more like him.

> So then, just as you received Christ Jesus as Lord, continue to live in him, rooted and built up in him, strengthened in the faith as you were taught, and overflowing with thankfulness.

> (Colossians 2:6–7)

1: Who Am I Really?

Mary Pytches

I recently watched an episode of the famous *Brat Camp* programme on Channel 4. I was struck by the behaviour and
language of the young girls sent out by their parents from
England to the Utah desert in a last-ditch attempt at
changing their self-destructive behaviour. One girl of
about 16 years of age confessed to the American therapist
that she was a regular cannabis user. 'That's who I am,'
she said several times. I think she was really saying that
she had lost her identity to such an extent that she only
felt she had found herself when she was in a drug-induced
haze. As I watched, amazed at such a sad and terribly mis-
taken admission, I wondered what had gone wrong in
that young girl's life to have caused her to lose herself in
such a dramatic way.

An important part of growing up is the discovery of
who we are apart from our parents, siblings, friends,

teachers and heroes. As small children we identify ourselves by our attachments, primarily to our parents. A baby looks up into its mother's eyes and on seeing love and joy there immediately feels OK inside. But on seeing disinterest or anxiety the message received is, 'I'm not OK.' Babies and small children are incredibly egocentric. Everything is about *them*. They don't have the maturity to understand that Mummy is a separate entity and has feelings that may have nothing to do with them. Therefore many times the bad feelings we have about ourselves begin at a young age. Living as we all do in a very broken world where nothing is perfect, it is almost inevitable that our emerging sense of self will be dented by those around us as we grow and develop. The answer is not to look for whom to blame, but to ask ourselves what can be done to regain the identity that God intended us to have. Understanding the reasons behind our struggle to find ourselves does not in itself bring healing, but it does give us a handle on solving the problem.

We all construct our identity using similar building blocks. As these fall into place our sense of self gradually develops. The first building block consists of the attachments we have, especially, as already mentioned, with our primary caregivers. Their treatment of us reveals to us what sort of person we are. They have the power to give us that sense of belonging that is vital to our security. Then, as we grow, the extended family plays its part. In these days when community life is on the wane and the extended family lives miles apart, this cementing of our links with others is often missing, leaving us with a longing to belong. In an attempt to fill the void and combat the sense of dislocation, young people search for a group to belong to which can give them a common identity.

Another important influence on our developing self is the culture into which we are born and in which we are nurtured. We lived for many years in South America, but when our oldest daughter Charlotte was 17, we came back to England so that our family could finish their education here. After nearly 30 years she returned to Chile for the first time and was surprised and delighted to find herself fitting back into the culture as if it were her own. 'Now I understand why I am like I am,' she said. The South Americans are effusive, friendly and extremely outgoing. They talk loudly, waving their hands around to make their point. It was as if Charlotte was rediscovering a part of herself that her English culture had almost squashed – though not quite! Where and when we are born is an important building block in developing a sense of self.

Other people's opinion of us is another factor. I grew up in north Devon and was fondly named 'a Devonshire dumpling' by my family and friends due to my healthy red cheeks and sturdy frame! Somehow that picture of myself has stuck in my mind and I am slightly surprised at times when I find myself not quite as robust as I imagine myself to be. It must be a picture that I have conveyed to other people, because recently, when I broke my arm, a friend rang and said how surprised he was to hear of the accident. 'We always thought you were indestructible,' he said. What other people say about us has a strong effect on our identity. We partly build the picture of ourselves through their eyes, especially the view of those close to us. I remember a young woman confessing to a terrible fear that no one would ever want to love her. 'I am so disgusting,' she said to my amazement. She was a clever, attractive person, but feared intimacy and kept people at arm's length. How could she feel so badly about herself, I wondered? Apparently, when she was a little girl her mother was always calling her disgusting. Twenty years later it was lodged so firmly in her mind that it affected her behaviour and attitude towards everyone around her. In *Victory over the Darkness* (Regal Books, 1992) Neil T. Anderson has said that no person can consistently behave in a way that is inconsistent with the way she sees herself. For a while we can keep it up, trying to be what we think other people want, but eventually our real, though hidden, self will surface and influence our behaviour. Most of us have had the experience of feeling like a split personality – one person on the outside for others to see, and another on the inside for our eyes only. We then live in fear that someone will discover that hidden part and reject us. Sadly the negative attitudes and cruel put-downs can stick in our minds long after other, more positive comments have been forgotten.

Attachments, culture and other people's opinions play a large part in identity formation, but the one we often put most emphasis on is our achievement. Anne Robinson, of *The Weakest Link* fame, said in her memoirs (*Memoirs of an Unfit Mother*, Time Warner Paperbacks, 2002), 'Here's the rub: who am I really? Friend of stars or the journalist, which is the real me? Hard to say!' Once again we see attachments, 'friend of stars', a building block in how she sees herself, but also her job, 'the journalist', playing a part in her identity. If we are asked to introduce ourselves to a group, most of us will answer either by naming someone to whom we are attached, or by saying what we do for a living. Joyce Meyer, an American TV preacher, recognises the danger of basing our self-image on something as insecure as an activity or an achievement. I once heard her say that we must learn to separate our 'who' from our 'do'. And yet many of us rely on our 'do' to give us that needed sense of significance.

Self-image is closely linked to our identity. For most of us, our physical appearance plays an important part in how we feel about ourselves. Not long ago I was in North America speaking at a conference full of well-dressed, middle-class people. Most of the women were well made up, with dyed hair, and a few with overly smooth faces rather suspiciously devoid of lines! Five minutes into my talk, my capped front tooth suddenly dropped from my mouth and, hitting the lectern, landed on the floor by my feet. 'Oh dear,' I lisped through the gaping hole, 'what am I going to do now?' Thinking frantically of the various options, I bent to pick it up. As I straightened up, a lady in the front row thoughtfully offered me a piece of her chewing gum. I gratefully accepted it and after chewing it stuck it around the tooth. Lo and behold, I was able to carry on with only an occasional need to push it back up into the socket. At the end of the talk, a woman of indeterminate age, but beautifully coiffured, came up to me. Clasping my hands in hers, she thanked me with tears in her eyes. 'You have so blessed me,' she said. I wondered which part of my talk had helped so much, until she added, 'You continued – you kept going.' I realised that the lady, whose appearance was so perfect, was in fact referring to the incident of the tooth! Whatever our age or sex, appearance plays an important part in how we see ourselves. In fact, I am amazed at how long my grandsons take to get ready to go out. It takes time, apparently, to get hair to stand on end!

Another building block in the formation of identity is the experiences of life we have had. Many of these are good and have the power to bless us and enhance our sense of value. It never ceases to amaze me how seemingly trivial incidents can stand out in a person's mind as important to their self-image. For instance, a young girl remembers that her dad once told her he liked what she was wearing, or another that her dad had taken her shopping and bought her some shoes. Inevitably it is our fathers who have the most impact on our developing image. It seems that however nurturing and encouraging our mothers are, they don't have the same impact on us as fathers do – especially in those vital teenage years. Conversely, there are those who have not had positive input from the adults around them and have even experienced events that have been negative and destructive to their self-worth. When a child is physically or sexually abused by an adult it leaves deep emotional scarring and a painful sense of shame. Their self-image has been tarnished. Only the mercy and love of God can wipe the slate clean, and reinstate that sense of worth that rightfully belongs to us all who have been made in his image.

Whether through our attachments, the culture around us, other people's opinions of us, our achievements or our experiences in life, these building blocks are the normal ways in which we develop a sense of who we are. These may be negative or positive, but they are usually a mixed bag for all of us. There is nothing wrong with any of them, except that they are incredibly unstable and open to change. Those near to us may move or even die, the world is forever changing, people alter their opinions of us, certainly our activities change with age, and our experience of life is never static. A young woman came to see me recently, having been forced to take sick leave because of stress. In the previous three months she had left college, moved into a new home, got married and started a new job, and then wondered why she was suffering a major identity crisis! Our sense of self can easily be threatened if these familiar building blocks change in any way. So how can we inject stability into our identity?

It is rather like the story in the Bible of the two builders. One man built his house on the sand, and when the rains and floods came and the winds beat against the house, it was in imminent danger of falling with a mighty crash. But the man who built his house on the rock, when the rain came in torrents and the floodwaters rose and the winds beat against that house, it didn't collapse (Matthew 7:24). Wherever we have built our identity on sandy foundations and changes come, as they surely will, the house is in danger of collapse. Somehow we have to discover how to build our identity on the unchanging word of God.

It is interesting to note that when Jesus was tempted in the wilderness, the devil challenged his identity three times with the words, 'If you are the Son of God. . .', 'If you are who you think you are. . .', and 'If you really are who God says you are. . .' But to each temptation Jesus responded with the words, 'It is written. . .', 'For it is written. . .', and 'It is also written. . .' The Scriptures hold the key to us finding a secure, unchanging foundation to our lives. It is in the Bible that we will discover who we really are. Jesus was in no doubt who he was and it affected everything he did. Before the Last Supper with his disciples he got up from the table, wrapped a towel around his waist and began to wash his disciples' feet. The text actually says that Jesus *knew* that his Father had given him authority over everything and that he had come from God and would return to God, and then comes the important little word '*so*' – '*so* he got up from the meal. . .' (John 13:4, italics mine). He knew exactly who he was, and with that truth firmly planted in his soul he was able to do the most menial of tasks without feeling in the least bit inferior or having his identity undermined.

When I was a child my family used to tease me gently by calling me 'The Little Accident'. It was true that I had arrived unexpectedly, well after my mother thought she had completed her family. It was never said in a cruel way, but nevertheless it sowed a seed of anxiety within me. As an adult I found my life hindered by a feeling that I was unwelcome or intruding on other people. I would joke that I needed a gold-lettered invitation card before I would call on anyone. I had been a Christian for many years without this feeling changing in any way, then one evening I was reading my Bible and the Holy Spirit highlighted some words to me in Colossians 3:12: 'Therefore, as God's *chosen* people, holy and *dearly loved*. . .' (italics mine). Suddenly I was filled with awe and joy as those words penetrated my mind and heart. It was still true that I may have been a mistake, but I realised in that instant that this was only part of the truth. My mother might not have planned to have me, but God had chosen to have me. He had purposed and planned for me to be born from the beginning of time. There is a truth that emerges in time and another that exists and emanates from eternity. We have a choice of ground on which to build our lives. One is unstable and insecure, but we are used to it: however painful it might be at times, it takes no effort to live there – we are completely at home with it. The other is unchangeable and firm as a rock, but it takes a disciplined decision to walk that way.

As we search the Scriptures and gradually store up in our hearts and minds a knowledge of who we are in Christ, we will find a wonderfully stable sense of security growing up within us. Then, whatever challenges or changes come our way, we will find we have been building our identity on an immovable and indestructible foundation.

2: The Names God Speaks Over Us

Ali MacInnes

A funny thing happened once I hit my mid-20s. My friends started mass-producing, having babies like it was going out of fashion! Over recent years it's been goodbye to the days of multiple engagements, wedding outfits and gift lists, and hello to 'No soft cheese and hold the wine, I'm pregnant'. And I've observed that alongside the inevitable joy of being with child comes the awesome task of deciding upon a suitable name. It's not a job to take lightly and friends who grew up longing for a child named 'River' have usually ended up opting for something a little more mainstream (such a bad joke!) as the responsibility sinks in. When faced with the fact that their choice will affect their little one for life, suddenly this is no small task. People want names with meaning, names that don't rhyme with rude things, names that don't remind them of mean teachers or naughty children, names that will suit a day-old screamer and a 90-year-old dear. Names matter. Our name is a label we can't avoid wearing. Incidentally, one baby name book told me that Alison (my real name) means 'Truthful Warrior Maid'. It fits well. My aim is to be more truthful and less frightened of conflict, and to make sure those around me know it's 'maid' as in 'female', not 'maid' as in 'make the tea'. Anyway, I digress. . .

My belief is that names matter to God – not necessarily the names we were given at birth (though he can use them), but there is a name that he speaks over us from heaven and our choice is whether we live in the strength of those names or in slavery to the names given to us by the world.

We see the importance of names in the Bible. Check out Abram in the book of Genesis. This guy has been promised by God that he will be a father – and not just to one child, but to many nations. The problem is that both he and his wife are getting on a bit and it doesn't seem possible. But God promises, and as if to back up his promise, or to underline it, he changes Abram's name to Abraham – which means 'Father of Many' (see Genesis 17).

Although that name seemed impossible by human standards, as we read on in Genesis we hear how his wife, Sarah, did in fact conceive and give birth to a son, Isaac, who in turn had twins, Jacob and Esau. Jacob produced (with the help of a few women) twelve sons who became the fathers of the twelve tribes of Israel, who became many nations. So for Abraham the name God gave him – though seeming impossible – was spot on.

We see this again in the life of Gideon, whom we read

about in Judges. At the time Gideon appears on the scene, God's people are having a tough time of it under the Midianites. They've been crying out to God to save them and he hears their cries: a messenger of the Lord appears to Gideon – someone who is so fearful of the bullying Midianites that he's threshing wheat from the safety of a winepress. The angel of the Lord addresses Gideon as 'Mighty Warrior'. He comes carrying a message from God, but it appears a mistake has been made because Gideon corrects him. He tells the angel that he is pretty much nothing – that he is the lowest and least of the lot and therefore definitely not a mighty warrior. But he is told to go in the strength he has and that the Lord will be with him. As Gideon steps out in obedience, he does defeat the Midianites and so we see (hindsight is a wonderful thing) that again, God is right. Gideon was addressed as 'Mighty Warrior' not because of how he felt, but because of who God created, called and equipped him to be.

My belief is that God is speaking to us about who we are and the names he has for us. It's not always easy for us to hear, because there are so many other labels that we find so much easier to wear – negative names we've picked up along the way through harmful words, bad experiences, failings and weaknesses. But it's our choice: will we listen to God, or to our own circumstances? Will we listen to God, or to the voice of our own insecurities, hang-ups and brokenness?

Before I get stuck into that any further, there's one other guy in the Bible I'd like to look at, someone else to whom God gave a name – and that's Peter, one of the twelve disciples.

In Matthew 16 we read about the moment when Jesus delivers Peter's heavenly name. Jesus has asked his disciples who the people say he is. They tell him that there are various rumours circulating: some say he's Elijah, some say Jeremiah, or one of the other prophets. When he asks who the disciples think he is, Peter pipes up, 'You are the Christ, the Son of the living God.' Well done, Pete! Go straight to the top of the class. Jesus says:

> Blessed are you, Simon son of Jonah, for this was not revealed to you by man, but by my Father in heaven. And I tell you that you are Peter, and on this rock I will build my church. . .

> (Matthew 16:17–18a)

So Simon Peter is christened 'The Rock' (long before WWF was ever even dreamed of). Admittedly that was a fairly good answer Peter gave. I reckon the other disciples were gutted they didn't come up with that answer, because it's definitely a ten-out-of-ten moment.

But Peter wasn't exactly consistent in star pupil behaviour and at times, as we read the Gospels, the idea of calling this slightly unstable, all-over-the-place guy 'The Rock' seems almost laughable. In fact, the Gospels are littered with classic 'Peter' moments, where he acts before thinking and opens his mouth without pausing (anyone relating to him?). For example, just after the 'Rock' incident, Jesus begins to explain 'The Plan' to his disciples: that he would go to Jerusalem, suffer many things, be killed and then be raised to life (Matthew 16:21). Peter is not happy: 'Never, Lord! . . . This shall never happen to you!' You can't blame Peter for his reaction – no one wants to hear their best friend talking that way. If we did, we'd send them off

for a good round of prayer ministry for speaking so negatively about themselves! But for Peter there could well
have been another disappointing dimension to Jesus'
plans: the Jews had been waiting for, longing for, a
Messiah to do away with the oppression they faced under
the occupying Romans. They didn't want a Messiah who
would die, but a Messiah who would do business, who
would rule and reign and get rid of the baddies.

Jesus has to correct Peter: 'Peter, get out of my way.
Satan, get lost. You have no idea how God works' (Matthew
16:23, *The Message*). That's a bit embarrassing. The Rock has
no idea how God works. And it gets worse. You can read
the story of Jesus' transfiguration in Matthew 17, but
here's the gist.

Jesus takes Peter, James and John up a mountain, Jesus
starts glowing, his clothes turn whiter than Daz white
and long-dead Moses and Elijah turn up for a chat. Now, I
could fairly easily be described as someone who talks a lot,
perhaps even as someone who talks too much, but I think
I could safely say that this little scene on the mountain
would have rendered me speechless. It's not exactly a run-
of-the-mill moment. But not Peter. He says, 'Lord, it is good
for us to be here. If you wish, I will put up three shelters –
one for you, one for Moses and one for Elijah' (Matthew
17:4). Talk about killing the moment! What on earth was
going through his mind when he asked that question?
Someone really should have taken him aside and taught
him the 'count to ten before speaking' rule.

And still it gets worse; still it gets more un-Rock-like.
Skip forward to the Garden of Gethsemane: Peter can't
keep his eyes open for an hour or two, even though his

friend and master asks him to. Even worse than that, there's the more than slightly awkward moment during Jesus' arrest when Peter cuts off some bloke's ear. Like *that* little gesture was going to help anyone! And as if Jesus didn't have enough on his plate in that moment without having to clear up after Peter's mess. . .

Then, of course, we have Peter's pièce de résistance, his denial when, as predicted by Jesus, he insists in the strongest possible terms that he doesn't know Jesus.

Reading about Peter is the one thing that makes me so glad I wasn't around in Jesus' time. Could you imagine someone being around to record all of your most embarrassing and ditsy moments? Mine would fill a book, a thick one. What makes it worse is that all this comes from the guy Jesus has named The Rock. With all these moments – ranging from the awkward to the downright disastrous – there must have been so many times when Peter questioned Jesus' knowledge, wisdom or authority in giving him such a name. Can you really use me? Are you sure you don't want to rethink? Do you think I'm someone I'm not?

The truth is that, in amongst the ear chopping and falling asleep, we do catch a glimpse of Peter the Rock. When Jesus walks on water (Matthew 14), Peter is the only one of the Twelve to get out on the water and give it a go. We think of his lack of faith and the fact that he started to sink, but I'm always amazed that he got out of the boat in the first place. It's that hot-headed courageousness, the heart of a man who wanted to be doing whatever Jesus was doing, no matter how crazy or scary, that gives us a taste of the church-planter to come. Maybe the sort of

Rock Jesus was looking for was someone who was not *dependable*, but *dependent*. Not perfect, but excited about what Jesus was doing and just wanting to be a part of it anyway.

We see that same desire in Peter's heart in the story of Jesus washing his disciples' feet (John 13). It's a pretty gross job in anyone's books, but especially when you've been wearing open sandals on dusty roads. And these are men's feet, remember – so we're not talking neat pedicures and girly scents. Think crusty skin, smelly bits, long, dirty nails. . . It was a job for the common entry-level servant, not for the faint-hearted and certainly not appropriate for the Saviour of the world. So of course Peter objects: 'No . . . you shall never wash my feet' (John 13:8). But Jesus is demonstrating something of infinite importance – this is servant leadership, a love that is humble. He says to Peter, 'Unless I wash you, you have no part with me.' 'Then, Lord,' Peter replies, 'not just my feet but my hands and my head as well!' (John 13:8b–9).

Yes, Peter often missed the point, got the wrong end of the stick, made mistakes and put his foot in it, but ultimately he just wanted to be in the thick of whatever Jesus was doing. He was on a path to maturity, and as we read on in the New Testament we begin to see a bit more of this Rock-like character coming out: someone who obediently waits for the infilling of the Holy Sprit; someone who fearlessly preaches the good news of Jesus and sees thousands coming to know God; someone who steers the baby church through those early teething issues. We see a wise and reasoned man, still not perfect, but someone who took the church forward with wisdom and passion, truly being the earthly rock on which Jesus built his church.

You see, all along God was right. God knew he was The Rock, and made the right decision in choosing Peter. Should we be surprised at this?

This brings me full circle: God gives all of us a name and we need to live under that rather than the names that we've given ourselves, or that life seems to have dished out to us along the way. We must live out the truth of who God says we are. First and foremost we hear this truth through the eternal Word of God, the Bible. Here are some of our names according to the Bible. They are general names that apply to all who belong to God, but the fact that they're general doesn't make them any less amazing. We are:

> Chosen (1 Peter 2:9);
> Made in his image (Genesis 1:27);
> Children of God (Romans 8:16);
> Loved (John 3:16; Romans 5:8; 8:35–39);
> Forgiven (Ephesians 1:7; 2:8–9);
> Valuable (Matthew 10:29–31);
> Friends of God (John 15:14–15);
> Delighted in (Zephaniah 3:17);
> New creations (2 Corinthians 5:17);
> Free (John 8:36);
> His (Isaiah 43:1).

Those are just some of the amazing things the Bible tells us about who we are in God. We have to learn to get this truth in our lives, literally to make the Bible our daily bread, the very thing that feeds and sustains us, and let the truth of who God says we are set us free.

So many of us have got used to listening to lies, but Jesus

said in John 8:32 that when we know the truth it will set us free. This is the truth to which we need to cling: that we are chosen, and therefore we haven't been forgotten, overlooked, abandoned or ignored. We're made in his image, therefore all the rubbish we believe about ourselves just can't be true. Each of us in some way reflects (albeit imperfectly) an almighty, amazing, beautiful, compassionate, wise, loving, creative God. We're his children, not mistakes but desired daughters. We're loved, not rejected; forgiven, not guilty; valuable, not worthless; friends of God, not servants, not one of a number or a face in the crowd; we're delighted in, not a burden to God, or someone he merely tolerates or puts up with. We're new creations, which means that in Christ we have a new DNA – we don't have to end up the way our parents did, or live as slaves to past mistakes. We're free – free from sin, free to love God and others, not slaves to life, death, the rat race, or to what others may tell us we are or are not. And we're his – we belong to him, he is glad to call us his own, and we get to spend eternity enjoying friendship with him.

A few years ago I met a lady who was at a crunch point in her life. She had been married for 15 years and every day her husband told her, faithfully and passionately, 'You're so beautiful, I love you so much, I'm so glad you're my wife,' but every day she brushed his words aside. She couldn't accept them, because she didn't believe him. What she actually believed was that she was worthless, ugly and unloved. She had felt that way about herself for as long as she could remember and, no matter what her husband said, she couldn't seem to believe anything different. Then God broke in. He'd been trying for years, trying to tell her that he called her Beautiful, Valuable and Loved. She was faced with a choice: would she continue to live in the place of pain, or would she choose to let go of her old names and take hold of, believe, live out the names God was calling her? She was so scared of letting go of the way she'd always seen herself – even though those names were damaging, they were also so familiar – but bravely she chose to ask God to take them away from her and to help her accept the way he sees her.

So often we give ourselves names like Worthless, Sinner, Unloved, but God is in heaven calling out something completely different. Although we might never say it aloud, it's there in our demeanour, the way we put ourselves down, our approach to life, our fears, the things that hold us back, the compliments we can't accept, those deep and secret thoughts we have about ourselves. And so it's as if we're going through life introducing ourselves, 'Hi, my name is Abandoned,' and God is saying, 'No, her name is Chosen! I choose her, I love her, I call her my own!' Or we say, 'Hi, my name is Useless, Unlovely, Insignificant, Rubbish. . .' and God says, 'No, she's Wonderful, she's Valuable, she's so Special to me. I made her in my image, and I love what I've created. I'm so glad to call her my friend.'

As well as these wonderful, general names, I also believe that, as with Abraham, Gideon and Peter, God wants to speak to us a specific name. Some of you have already heard his whisper. You've heard it, but not yet dared to believe that he is calling you. It can be so hard to believe God when the circumstances of our lives or the stuff in our past seem so contrary to what he is saying.

Years ago, through a couple of minor workplace disasters, I gave myself the name Failure. Although I wasn't consciously aware of it for many years, my feelings and belief that I was destined to mess up coloured everything I was and all I tried to do. Because I believed myself to be Failure, I couldn't accept the other specific things God was calling me to. How could God trust me with anything if I was only going to fail and let him down and, even worse, make a fool of myself in the process? So, like Moses, I had lots of conversations with God along the lines of 'Get someone else to do it'. Then one day I was reading through my old journals and again and again I saw how many times God had spoken to me and, though I had faithfully recorded his words, ultimately I had just ignored them. As I read and reflected, I just cried. I hadn't realised till then how rebellious I had been. I thought I was justified in telling God I was no good for the job, but in answering God back or ignoring him I was being disobedient and missing out on so many good things he had for me. It was time to repent, to choose to let go of that name of Failure and begin to trust God. He is always right when he speaks and will always equip us for the things to which he calls us (Hebrews 13:20–21). Our weakness is no barrier to him – in fact, his strength is made perfect in our weakness (2 Corinthians 12:9). Our job is simply to get on and live those lives of obedience in response to his call.

When God gives us a name, we need to listen to him. He made us, and he knows who we really are and what we can do in his strength. When he tells us he can and wants to use us, we can trust him to be right, no matter what we might think or what the circumstances might seem to say.

God called Gideon a 'Warrior' when he was weak and afraid, he called Abraham a 'Father' of nations when he was childless and Peter a 'Rock' when he appeared to be anything but. For us, as with these men, what really matters and makes the difference is not what life is dishing out, or how we feel about ourselves, but who God says we are. We need to face the lies we've been living with and hand them over to him. It might not be easy or come naturally, and it might be that we have to lay these names down more than once, but as we do so we find the freedom to listen to and live out the life-giving, beautiful, freeing names he speaks over us.

Who does God say you are?

God at Work

Clare's Story

I am so grateful for what God has done in my life over the years. The biggest struggle and battle has been to break the fear of rejection. I found it so difficult to really believe in my heart that Jesus loved and accepted me unconditionally. As a child I always felt 'different'. I didn't fit in with the girls at school, because I loved to be active in playing sports, getting dirty and being adventurous and so I grew up as a tomboy. I suppose as a child you process the feeling of being different as something being wrong with you. The nagging voice and background noise was that I wasn't good enough and that I wasn't the daughter my parents wanted. The core question of my heart was: Am I beautiful? Am I good? Am I accepted? Am I OK?

I longed for my mum and dad to reassure me, but my parents had a difficult marriage which created an environment of insecurity. This was when my search for affirmation and love began. For most of my school and teenage life I threw myself into being good at everything – good grades, captain of various sports, and drama. I had many friends and sought affirmation through popularity and achievement. On the outside I was successful and popular, but inside I felt a failure and lonely, too afraid to expose what was really in my heart.

I also made an inner vow not to show weakness or vulnerability, in order to protect myself from more rejection. I tried to control and make my life so safe that I gave no one the chance to hurt me, so I became tough, independent and self-sufficient. I also became very driven and struggled to feel at peace, not really knowing a place of rest. My longing for love and acceptance also manifested itself in a series of sexual relationships with both men and women throughout my teenage years.

It was during my early 20s that the Lord took hold of my life and began to deal with my heart. As he began to speak his love directly and through others, the hardness of my heart and the self-protective walls began to fall as I felt the grief and hurt of my past. The shame and guilt of my sin fell away and I felt the affirmation of my Father in heaven. The Lord brought memories to mind of all the people I needed to forgive. I could never remember my dad telling me he loved me or picking me up and consequently had judged him as being passive and weak, but as I forgave and released him from my judgements, God was able to pour out his grace and healing. I forgave my mum for the times I had felt crushed and misunderstood and again the Lord healed painful memories and began to restore those lost years. He revealed himself as both mother and father to me and reconciled me to my natural parents.

I had to go through a time of deep repentance and take to the cross of Jesus all my self-protective ways. At the cross I renounced my vow of independence and ungodly belief that vulnerability was a weakness instead of a strength. I had to take steps back towards community and accountable relationships, instead of living in isolation for fear of needing people and trusting people. It became a daily decision not to be ruled by fear, instead choosing to let people see who I really was.

God has really broken the fear of rejection in my life, so that I can be confident in the woman he has made me to be. I struggled so much to get close to people and trust them, both peers and leaders, and thought I needed to protect my heart. I had trained myself to shut down, to shut down emotion, softness and tenderness. In doing so I lost the innocence of loving without fear. The fear also stopped others loving me, as I could only give so much of myself before the barriers would come up.

Now I know that whatever struggle or situation I find myself in, the love of Jesus is stronger. He can always reach me and find me. The question and fear I had growing up of being a 'mistake' – and wondering whether anyone really saw me and liked what they saw – was answered as Jesus revealed himself as lover and friend who knows me, created me and continues to enjoy me. I heard the affirmation of the Father saying, 'This is my daughter; I am so proud of her.' The lie that I needed to prove myself and earn the love of God and others was exposed, and the burden to succeed constantly and never fail was broken. What I experienced was God's love that set me free to love others instead of being self-conscious or fearful.

Before I became a Christian I often had seasons of depression, as I knew there was more to life than what I was experiencing. Since I became a Christian, that hunger has only increased, as I now know that I was longing for the kingdom of God: a kingdom full of love, hope and life, without sickness and sorrow. He has really blessed me with a wonderful community that is loving and accepting and that seeks to bring reconciliation and healing to others. I love the fact that God takes the foolish things, the broken lives like mine, and makes something beautiful from them.

3: Do You Fancy a Coffee Sometime?

Jo Saxton and Sally Breen

Meet Jo Saxton:

How hard could it be to get a man? In the end *someone* comes along, right? I'd go travelling, get established in my career, and then he'd sweep me off my feet and we'd live happily ever after. Except it wasn't that easy. I thought I'd tried everything. I tried looking for Mr Right, but he wasn't anywhere to be found. I tried *not* looking for Mr Right, and (surprise, surprise) I didn't find him then either. I had loads of guy friends, but I was always their 'sister'. So I tried being distant and alluring . . . and they kept their distance! I'd sought the Lord and thought I got prophetic words about 'The One'. Until they married someone else. I got together with my girlfriends and prayed for God to send us men of God. And I went to their weddings. I decided to wait, and nothing happened. I was gutted. I went to a fantastic church with masses of young adults, but it made no difference. It seemed as if we were all stuck.

Meet Sally Breen:

St Thomas's Church in Sheffield had hundreds of young adults. Eighty per cent of the church was under the age of 40. This generation were amazing at forming friendships and building community. Socials, retreats, parties, something was always going on. However, the staff team noticed that relationships never went further than friendships. It wasn't that people didn't want it; there were lots of conversations about meeting Mr or Miss Right. They just didn't do anything about it. Many of this generation had grown up with the heartache of broken homes and loveless marriages. They determined not to be another statistic. If they were going to take a step, it had to be a sure thing; they had to feel safe.

We could see that, as a result of all this, some of our young adults were way too idealistic, with expectations that came more from Hollywood than from biblical principles! Others were so locked into the 'friends' zone that they couldn't be bothered to move out of it. Yet the friends they loved so much could never be anything more. How could they fancy them? Many weren't prepared to take responsibility and be proactive in this area of their lives. It felt too weird, even wrong. We are spiritual, emotional and physical beings, but in relationships we saw that often one of these dimensions was out of kilter. Relationships in our church were overspiritualised. There was a lot of praying about it, but very little action.

As a staff team we realised that this was a huge spiritual battle. This wasn't just about matchmaking; we all saw and dealt with the casualties of this battle on a regular basis. Some were broken by loneliness, some left the church when they fell in love with someone who didn't share their faith. In the months that followed we prayed, we taught on relationships, and we gave practical teaching on dating and directly encouraged people who liked each other to get together. Sometimes people just needed a kick in the right direction! Slowly people began to take risks and started dating. And yes, I went to loads of weddings!

Jo:

The Bible doesn't give direct dating advice, so I wasn't sure what to think. After a few years of getting nowhere, I turned to Sally Breen for help. She was the vicar's wife – maybe we could go for coffee and talk.

On the surface we were very different. She had grown up in middle-class suburbia; I was from inner-city London. She's white; I'm black. She's into New Country music; I think New Country sucks. She'd got married at 21; I was 20-something and hadn't been on a date for years. Maybe she didn't seem like the obvious choice of person to talk to about singleness. But I knew a lot about being single! And while I had some wonderful single girlfriends, we spent a lot of time talking about men over a tub of Häagen-Dazs and going round in circles. I needed to try a different angle.

So we'd head out to a coffee shop, but we'd always bump into someone I didn't want listening in on my dirt! So most of these deep and meaningful conversations took place in the profoundly spiritual car parks of garden centres in Sheffield. For the next few years I laughed, sobbed, swore, hit the dashboard, sulked, listened and argued as I thrashed out this stuff with Sally. And Sally invested years in challenging my socks off while torturing me with her music.

Just imagine yourself now in the back seat with your Starbucks and be thankful it wasn't you!

If you're single and loving it, please don't feel pressured by this chapter. You *can* be single and complete with a great life! You don't need to justify it or explain it away. But if singleness hurts like nothing you've ever known, then read on.

We hope that telling you this story helps you in yours. And we'll pause every so often and ask you a few questions, just so that you're still part of the conversation. So, have you got your coffee?

In the film *Something New* (Universal Studios, 2006) Kenya, a successful African-American lawyer, is out with her girlfriends talking about Mr Right. Kenya insists that she isn't too picky about guys, but 'He's got to have a job . . . college education . . . no children, and not be bisexual. . .' Kenya's expectations are turned upside down when she meets a man who isn't the African-American executive ideal, but a white gardener. . .

I insisted I didn't have a list, I just knew what I wanted. He had to be a couple of years older than me, on fire for God, taller than me. He had to be a leader, because I was one. He had to know the Bible. He had to be able to sing. There needed to be a spark, I had to fancy him. It wasn't a list, it was my 'type'.

Sally said, 'Joannah, you look at all the older leaders you admire and want the guys in your life to be like that now. But the guys you admire weren't like that in their 20s! You need to look at their potential. This list just isn't reality.'

'But I can't help what I'm attracted to, Sal!'

And in one sense I was telling the truth. I couldn't help it. I was done with mistakes and heartache. If I was going to take the risk, it had to be . . . perfect. Remember the song by Fairground Attraction?

I didn't realise just how much films, novels and love songs had shaped my expectations! My list was a fantasy to protect me from getting hurt again. This guy would heal my insecurities. He would make me feel beautiful and whole. He would say, 'You complete me,' and adore cute kids, just like Jerry Maguire. He'd be my Mr Darcy. And we'd live happily ever after in Christian ministry, changing the world together.

I hated it when guys told me they wanted a blonde, size ten wife, who would support their ministry. Other than the fact that it screamed 'Not *you*, Joannah!', it seemed shallow. I didn't want the pressure of living up to some criteria to be good enough to go out with. Yet I didn't see the hypocrisy in my frustration. I was doing *exactly* the same thing. They may have wanted a trophy wife, but I wanted a trophy husband – it just looked different and sounded spiritual.

Have you noticed that our lists – girls or guys – never have the tough stuff from everyday life? They don't include an active sexual history, eating disorders, dysfunctional in-laws and a special request for major PMT. I wanted someone who could rescue me, protect me and accept my weaknesses and brokenness while having none of his own.

Over time Sally helped me to see what my list was based on. Wounds that only God could heal, fears that only God's love could cast out. A bit of vanity here, a bit of worldliness there. Behind my ideal stood the *idol* of the perfect guy and the painless relationship. In the Bible God is consistent about idols, these man-made constructions to which we give all our emotional energy and love. He tells us to get rid of them, that they get in the way of the real thing: 'Those who cling to worthless idols forfeit the grace that could be theirs' (Jonah 2:8).

It was tough letting go. . .

But God finally got a chance to heal some wounds, and I began to stop expecting a guy to do it all.

- What's on your list and why?
- What has shaped your expectations?
- Are there idols you need to get rid of?

Sally:

Sometimes what happens amongst young adults is that, even though people aren't dating or going out, they get involved with one another emotionally. So while physically nothing is going on, the relationship is so intense that they get into bed with each other emotionally. They spend time chatting on the phone or the internet, texting or going out to the movies or for dinner. There are deep and meaningful conversations, shared secrets, openness and vulnerability. Friends with (emotional) benefits! Yet because some of their needs are already being met, they don't take it to the next step. In the end one of them goes out with someone else, and the one left behind is upset, confused and angry.

Jo:

I met this guy and we clicked straight away. We hung out a lot, spent hours talking on the phone. It was a long-distance thing so we spent time, money and effort seeing each other and had a great time. However, I wasn't sure where I stood with him. I don't think we even held hands. We called it many things: 'great relationship', 'significant friendship', 'special connection'. But it was never called 'going out'. Sometimes I felt incredibly special, other times totally alone. It couldn't go on. When I asked, 'Where do you see this going?' he couldn't say. He didn't want to let go of what we had, but he didn't want to take it further. Yet. Maybe in the future. Let's just see. I needed a coffee!

'You could commit to him and choose to wait,' Sally began, 'but you can't expect anything from him. He could turn around one day and say he loves you, or fall in love with someone else.'

'I don't think I can do that, Sal. Any other options?'

'You could walk away and stay away.'

'Great options.'

I walked away, and it felt like a break-up. How did I get there in the first place? Well, when all my friends were getting married, it felt like I had someone. Someone who was at least a bit mine, and people would ask if I was 'seeing' him. It felt better than no one asking anything at all. I liked the feeling of at least being wanted a bit. And for a while that was enough. For a while.

- Does this sound familiar?
- Are you involved emotionally or physically with someone, but not going out with them?
- Do you have 'friends with benefits'?

The dating advice Mike and Sally gave transformed the church. There was an explosion of weddings! Friendships changed. People moved on, couples hung out together. I'd find new single friends and they'd meet people too! But nothing was happening for me. I'd prayed and fasted, and still there was *nothing*. I'd done spiritual warfare. I'd stood in faith, confessed my doubts. I'd sobbed my heart out at 4 a.m. in my room. *Nothing*. Tomorrow was just another day.

'Sally, what's wrong with me? Is it because I'm black? Because I'm a leader? No one wants to be with me, so there must be something wrong with me!'

'That's a lie, Joannah. You need to take those thoughts captive and throw them away.'

'Maybe God doesn't like me.'

'Joannah, he loves you. You need to stand on the truth, not your feelings, or the lies.'

'But Sal, everyone else is getting together! Why them and not me?'

'Comparison is death. It's just not worth it. This is not a competition, and when you compare yourself to others, all it does is make it worse.'

'But it's so hard, Sal. It's not fair. . .'

Proverbs 13:12 says, 'Hope deferred makes the heart sick,' and I had a severe case of heart-sickness. Standing on the truth that God loved me and is always faithful was the last thing I felt like doing. I had a simple choice to make. I could cling to God, put him first and accept that my dreams were not my rights, or I could try to work it out on my own. Some friends in a similar position met guys who weren't Christians and eventually left the church. Once I'd have been judgemental, but by now I understood some of the frustration and pain behind those choices. In the end, I chose differently.

Things *not* to say to a single woman on a bad day:

- 'You'll find someone when you're not looking. . .'
- 'I just prayed about it and I met X the next day. . .'
- 'Maybe you're called to be single. . .'

These were the statements that made me want to commit acts of violence.

I'd put my life on hold waiting for Mr Right long enough. I'd convinced myself it was the spiritual thing to do, to patiently wait on God and seek him. The only problem was, I knew from theological study that phrases like 'waiting on God' and 'seeking God' did not involve doing nothing until God turned up. They were active phrases, where you prayed *and* got on with your life, walking with God. Maybe Sally and Mike had a point about being proactive. It got me thinking. I decided to take my life back and do all the things I'd planned to do when I got married. I got a new car. I worked towards buying a house. I led mission trips and travelled the world. I sponsored a child with Compassion International. I hung out with single and married friends and enjoyed them all. I was myself again and it felt fantastic. I began to make the most of the fun and freedom of being single. Maybe because I was generally more relaxed, I even went on a couple of dates.

> If you're happy and you know it, find a strapline. When people ask you about singleness, always have your one-liner ready:
>
> • Sally's suggestion: 'I'm really happy with my life at the moment! How's yours?'
> • Jo's suggestion: 'So many men, so little time.'

Sally:

In our relationships talks, we gave simple guidelines for healthy dating. Here is a brief summary:

- Get to know some people of the opposite sex. Hang out socially in groups. You need to be in community to meet people.
- If you want to get to know one of these guys better, go on a date. This is understood by both parties to be just a date, not a proposal of marriage or an invitation into bed. If you enjoy the date, do it again!
- Normally by the third date you need to decide if you want to go out with each other. Otherwise it's easy to get emotionally involved and dependent without a commitment. If you don't want to go out with that person, then say so. If you do – say so!

Jo:

Sally encouraged me to ask guys out on dates. At first I thought this was ridiculous and theologically suspect, but I changed my mind. Here's why. Why waste time obsessing over a guy for weeks, trying to read the situation and looking daggers at every girl he talks to, when you could just ask him out for a coffee? When Ruth met Boaz on the threshing floor, she wasn't asking for a cup of sugar; she asked him to marry her (Ruth 3:9). If she can rise to the occasion to get her man, can we really not do a coffee?

Now life still had its disappointments and lonely days. But that's life, isn't it? What made it so great was that it was healthy and normal. When Jesus talked with his disciples about the anxieties they faced going through life, he told them, 'Seek first his kingdom and his righteousness, and all these things will be given to you as well' (Matthew 6:33). I was putting God first, and learning to develop a healthy approach to relationships. As a result I was blessed.

- In what ways have you put your life on hold because you are waiting for your husband?
- Are you willing to go out on a few dates?
- Could you do a 'Ruth' and ask a man out?

I was finally more secure. I had my friendships, my community, my work and travels, and I got comfortable. There was no room in my life for a guy, no space for a relationship. And I liked it. No risks, no hurt. Maybe I could adopt a child. Eventually I felt God challenge me that if I ever wanted to get married, then I'd have to change. Change?

DO YOU FANCY A COFFEE SOMETIME?

Change? I'd burned my list and killed my idols. I'd stopped those emotional entanglements and taken hold of my life. I'd cleaned up the past and moved on. What else was there to do?

Go for coffee.

Sally was blunt. I had grown spiritually, healed emotionally, which was great. But if I wanted to get married as much as I said I did, it was time to get totally practical.

We looked at my image, how I presented myself. I was stuck in a casual, comfy rut. I didn't need a revolution, but Sally suggested things like accessories, and maybe exchanging my tattered but beloved Adidas shell-tops for some kitten heels. Then we looked at my body language and how I spoke. I was so busy trying to show that I enjoyed being single that no one knew I wanted to get married! I wasn't vulnerable. I needed to acquire a few skills.

She hadn't finished: 'You need to meet more men. What about a Christian dating agency? Or an Oak Hall holiday?'

I nearly choked. 'Sally, that's a bit desperate, don't you think?'

'Who cares? Desperate and single, desperate and married – what would you prefer? If everything works, you won't care how you got together. What does it matter what anybody else thinks?'

'So you don't think it's a bit weird?'

'What have you got to lose?'

Eight years without a snog. She had a point.

'And one more thing. If anyone – *anyone* – asks you on a date, you go.'

There was no escape, Sally was holding me accountable

WORTH KNOWING

to sharpen up my image and get more proactive. I called the dating agency. I considered lying when they asked my name. It cost more than I could afford at the time, so I offered to get involved at New Wine that year in the young adults' tent instead! Same thing, right?

Maybe some of you are choking at how superficial this all sounds, but when was the last time you fell for a guy who dressed badly and had BO and poor social skills? He could have been the next Billy Graham, Bill Gates, Brad Pitt or Bono underneath, but admit it, he wouldn't have got a second look. Appearances aren't everything, but they do matter. And I guess I was desperate to meet someone, but you know what? It's not an unforgivable sin! Admitting it finally made me exchange my introspection for some radical action.

- How do you come across to the opposite sex?
- Have you got too comfortable?
- Would you be willing to get out there to meet more people? A dating agency? Speed dating? A blind date?

Then one day, as CeCe Peniston said, 'Finally it happened to me, right in front of my face, my feelings can't describe it. . .'

I went on a mission trip to Germany. When I returned, one of the mission team asked me out on a date. I was in complete shock. He was friendly, a good laugh, but I didn't fancy him. I didn't notice a spark between us. He was different from my normal choices, five years younger, an engineer, an ordinary guy. I decided to try reality for a change, the guy right in front of me. Best decision I've ever made. He turned out to be the love of my life. And without the process of change through which God had led me, and a helping hand (more like a kick) from Sally, the chance would have passed me by.

I'll be upfront with you. I have very little to share on the whole going out phase, because we got engaged after five weeks. That's right, five weeks. But there's one question I'm always asked: how did you *know* after only five weeks?

God never spoke to me verbally saying, 'Marry him.' But everything about our relationship shouted out God's blessing. 'Hope deferred makes the heart sick, but a longing fulfilled is a tree of life' (Proverbs 13:12). This relationship was like a source of life to me. It was fun, healing and healthy. We argued, we talked. We dreamed dreams, we watched the World Cup. It was extraordinarily ordinary. He was open, honest and committed to me. He loved me. People we loved and respected supported us. I thought of life with him and without him. And I decided I preferred it with him. We were aware that at five weeks our relationship was immature and that there was plenty of room to grow. We just decided we wanted to grow and do life together.

I'm not saying everyone should know that quickly! I have plenty of friends who got engaged much further along into the relationship. Some of us make the commitment and work out the details later; some work out the details to make the commitment.

That said, it still took some getting used to. I'd been single for eight years. I was used to doing my own thing, my friends, my community. I missed being single. I'd left my family home years before, but still I had to make room in my heart and life to work at this new adventure. Sometimes it felt so unfamiliar that giving up would have been the easy option. But neither of us wanted to do that. So we didn't.

> • Are you willing to take a risk and be open to dating someone completely different?

There's always a huge gulf between reality and the Hollywood-inspired fantasies about love and life. We're a generation who've been sold the lie that not only can we 'have it all', but it's our God-given right and natural expectation. And when it comes to love, our expectations often reach their peak and we shoot for the stars! Yet sometimes we miss out on opportunities or get disappointed, because our reality often doesn't look like the fantasy we've held in our hearts for so long.

I've been married for three years now, and while I'm no veteran I've certainly learned a lot so far. Once the wedding and honeymoon are over, what next? Well . . . life! Everyday, ordinary life. You learn how to communicate with each other, how to work out your finances, your time and your conflicts. You learn to forgive and be forgiven. You choose to love, when it doesn't flow freely. You learn to lay down your own individual dreams and instead dream dreams together. You work out priorities and make sacrifices, even when it hurts. You learn to walk with God together, but also to keep your own relationship with God fresh. There's still Monday morning and going to work, bills to pay, and a house to clean. There are life's highs and lows, and those simply average days. You still have other important relationships and commitments. There's your family, your single and married friends, your small group, your church – they don't disappear with the ring!

And like it or not, even the insecurities and weaknesses that existed before marriage rise again. You're still you, and he's still him!

So three years in, I've learned that the list really doesn't matter. When you're staring your bills in the face and you aren't sure how you'll make ends meet, your husband's height doesn't matter. When we were in the emergency room uncertain of our baby's health, then my husband's calling, taste in music and academic achievements really weren't the issue. We have an eight-month-old baby. When do we have time to go clubbing so I can check out my husband's dance moves?

So what do you need for the journey when you're navigating your way through this part of your life? A firm grasp on reality, a firm grasp on the Lord – and a firm friend who will remind you of both these things.

- Someone who'll keep you grounded and help you laugh at yourself.
- Someone who'll tell you that comparing yourself to others is a waste of time.
- Someone who'll encourage you to embrace 'life in all its fullness' whatever your marital status.
- Someone who's always got time for a coffee.

4: Woman in the Workplace

Michele Guinness

I don't remember ever saying to myself, 'This is a new era for women. Go out and get it all – career, kids, church leadership, a disciplined spiritual life, a beautiful home, hospitality, leisure, and a perfect body!' Just as well. No disappointment there, then.

In fact, when the children did come along, I was delighted to kiss youth work goodbye. I'd never envisaged it becoming a career, but didn't know what else to do. The fact that the church in those days tutted at mums who abandoned pre-school children for the job market gave me a great excuse to play the stereotypical Christian wifey – leader of women's ministry, pusher of buggy, maker of quiches, Oxfam-shopper, and husband's shadow.

But oh, was I bored! To prevent my brain from deserting me in disgust, I began to write – articles, books, radio scripts – and, miracle, kept being asked for more. Whenever the children were at playschool or asleep, late at night or in the early hours of the morning, I slaved over a hot word processor. I still didn't set my sights too high. One day, in that state of semi-reverie that praying can sometimes be, I said, 'When the children are older, I'd really like to be a television researcher, maybe finding art deco sets for *Poirot*.' Within weeks the phone rang, and I was offered a full-time job as a researcher at ITV – in religious programmes, not *Poirot*. 'What about childcare? How will we manage?' I said to Peter, my husband. 'We will,' he reassured me. 'When the door opens, walk.'

On my first morning I sat at an empty desk, totally devoid of self-confidence, pushing a blank piece of paper around. But instinct kicked in and research led to scripting, scripting to presenting, and presenting, eventually, to a career in PR.

Thanks to yet another almighty shove from my beloved husband, I find myself 20 years later Head of Communications for a Strategic Health Authority, with a team to manage and around 30 communications managers in NHS trusts across a wide area to advise and support, not to mention providing regular briefings for MPs, health ministers and even Number 10. And this is the woman who never wanted a career! I have been out of my depth many times, befuddled by jargon and concepts beyond my ability to grasp, terrified of showing my ignorance, convinced I'd be unmasked as a fraud who really didn't know anything about the theory of communications, and totally dependent on a wisdom far greater than mine. 'Oh Lord,' I have cried, at Board or Department of Health meetings, confronted with forests of unintelligible papers, all in NHS gobbledegook, 'I don't understand a word of this, but you do. Please translate – and put something half convincing in my mouth when I'm asked to respond.' To my amazement, he does!

I have discovered that the best option is to be me – management-speak free – but passionate about the quality of care patients receive. This is the vision rekindled in my spirit every morning long before I get to work, when I wish I'd gone to bed sooner and slumber through the Scriptures with a steaming mug of coffee, praying that God will reignite my passion for what I'm called to do, and give me the opportunity and wisdom to do it. 'Dog tiredness', I once read, 'is such a lovely prayer.'

From Monday to Friday, for between eight and ten hours a day, most of us live in a parallel universe, unknown to everyone except our work colleagues. We occupy environments that have their own rules, behaviours, language and foibles. My workplace consists of offices of five or six people who sit in front of computer screens, directing the machinations of the NHS by email. We rarely get up to speak to each other (why bother when you can speak electronically?), only go to the loo when desperate (why don't we use catheters?) and know the only real excitement of the day is finding dried and curled-up sandwiches in the kitchen left over from a meeting (saves going out to buy them). This weird universe is our natural habitat for most of our life, yet on Sundays, for all the recognition it gets from the Christian community, it might not even exist. But by the evening service, inadvertently, I'm often wandering there in my mind – alone. I long to describe it to my friends, tell them what I have to face the following day, share my fears and longings, invite their prayers, but the problem is that Christians like to divide their lives into boxes – what is spiritual and what is not. Church is spiritual, home group is spiritual, but the unspoken message we often receive is that our workplace is not. Yet this place is my life for most of the week. This tiny patch is my inheritance – for now. This is where I'm called to bring the kingdom of God.

Standing at the photocopier one day, trying hard not to resort to the language of my colleagues in face of its usual contrary behaviour, I was joined by Bev, PA to one of the directors, who had become a Christian a few weeks earlier. It had begun with a pre-Christmas invitation to a Riding Lights Christian theatre show, mulled wine and mince pies, and ended with her inviting herself to an Alpha course in our church. There we were, chatting about Sunday, when along came the boss's PA, who told us she kept hearing a voice.

'Do you know where these words are from?' she asked. 'Because I haven't a clue, and yet they're familiar somehow.'

She proceeded to quote virtually the entire Sermon on the Mount – more than I could ever remember off by heart. Bev and I gawped at her.

'That's Jesus,' we said.

'What does he want with me?' she asked.

'Your life?' we suggested.

Work is a gift from God, given at creation for the satisfaction and enjoyment of human beings, who instinctively reflect the creativity of the Creator. Enter rebellion and self-righteousness, and up come the thistles and briars. Till becomes toil, and feels like it on a Monday

WORTH KNOWING

morning. We are left with the paradox set out in the book of Ecclesiastes: 'What I have seen to be good . . . is to eat and drink and find enjoyment in all the toil with which one toils under the sun the few days of his life which God has given him' (Ecclesiastes 5:18, RSV).

We love the creativity but loathe the relentlessness, relish the satisfaction but resent the frustrations, enjoy the significance but hate it when we are taken for granted, need the financial benefits but are destroyed by the stress. The preacher's point is that since work has to be done – and it is a temporary arrangement for this life only, no matter how tedious – we should enjoy its rewards and find what fun in it we can.

According to the New Testament, that fun includes being a servant. Cleaning mounds of filthy coffee cups left in the communal kitchen sink, doing the photocopying and running errands does not come naturally, either because we feel we're being put upon, or because it's beneath us as a manager. Yet nothing was too menial for the Servant King who gave up his power and glory to live with lowly humans, washing their smelly feet when the working day had made them mucky. And colleagues do notice when we serve them graciously and willingly, without Uriah Heep-like wringing of hands, or resorting to the facial expression of someone who has just bitten into their first olive.

There are times when I have to pull rank – when I'm not getting the performance from my team that I have the right to expect, but more often to protect them from the unacceptable demands or expectations of another manager or colleague. Both seem to me to be in keeping with the Jesus approach. On occasions like that, a little power-dressing doesn't hurt. In fact, to be taken seriously women have to look as if they mean business – without being threatening. Personally, I like the way a small frill or piece of lace peeping out of a sharp suit combines approach-ability with the message 'don't mess with me'!

Being a servant doesn't mean letting your employer or colleague use you as a doormat. It doesn't mean submitting to bullying, harassment or exploitation. Buried in the Bible is an employment code of practice, now enshrined in law: wages must be paid on time, workers should not be expected to work longer hours than they are contracted to do, and health and safety are paramount. If an employer is not fulfilling their ethical duty, it may take a Christian to stand up to them and gently but firmly put the employee's point of view. When Jesus told us to turn the other cheek, he wasn't advocating weakness. A man or woman would only ever slap their slave across the face. Offering the other cheek is saying to a bully, 'Treat me like a slave, would you? Then slap me again and make a real fool of yourself.' In other words, this was powerful passive resistance.

Challenging oppressive systems or unacceptable behaviour is never easy. It involves risk – unpopularity, victimisation or even dismissal. Jesus certainly experienced the first two, and I suppose crucifixion was the ultimate dismissal. There are times, if the situation becomes really nasty and our mental health is threatened, when we may have to pack up our belongings and go. There is no shame in it and, even if we are pursued by inner accusations of inadequacy and failure, no reason not to walk out of the door with our head up. In one job I failed to report sexual harassment by a line manager, naively protecting the man's wife rather than my colleagues. He was suspended, of course, when another woman's infuriated husband finally shopped him, after he had made dozens of women's lives a misery. In another job, my favourite of them all, I suddenly found that my friendship with a very senior manager, who happened to be a Christian, was being used to accuse her of favouritism. In the end the only way to save her integrity was to hand in my notice. It cost me many tears, but at least I knew it was the honourable action this time.

I have also been sacked – the usual scenario, a new chief officer who wanted to bring in his own team. But no matter how much I told myself it was nothing to do with my performance, it was an enormous blow to my pride and self-worth. I was left with two choices: to blame the new head, rant and rage against him and inflict on him as much damage as my tongue was capable of doing, or accept the situation as a gift from God's hands because he had a new adventure up his sleeve for me, and take my leave with dignity in silence. I opted for the latter – and it half-killed me. I virtually had to clamp my tongue between my thumb and first finger, but a few weeks later my former PA rang me.

'It's like a battlefield here,' she said. 'Corpses everywhere as the sackings continue, and such screaming and crying in the corridors. Now, you didn't do that,' she added. 'We've all commented on it. Presumably it had something to do with your faith, did it?'

My husband Peter got another parish elsewhere in the

country, and I had my new adventure. The chief officer dropped dead in the work car park. His stress was manifestly greater than mine.

The prevailing cynicism in the workplace often makes it a difficult culture for the Christian, but moaning about management, back-biting, snide remarks and all the other potentially destructive little weapons of insecurity and one-upmanship should be shunned with disciplined determination. The respect for authority advocated by the apostle Paul is rare. There is an old Chinese saying I love: 'Never criticise someone until you've walked in their moccasins.' I would make a brilliant chief executive – in my dreams! In reality, I'd probably experience meltdown in a week and end up flat on my back in the work car park.

For the Christian, relationships matter. Common courtesy in the workplace is very uncommon. Grievances (and I have had one brought against me simply for doing my job as a manager) must be sorted out with as much openness and honesty as we can muster, confronting both unjustified and unpalatable truths about ourselves. Receiving criticism is desperately hard, but I learned early, from a wonderful and gracious role model, that nothing gives us such an opportunity to grow. And God intends us to grow – from one degree of glory to another.

Can we have it all? In many ways, I think we can – but not all at once. A friend of mine who has just become dean of a university medical school gave up any hope of marriage or children 20 years ago when she became a consultant obstetrician and gynaecologist. That was her choice then. It might have been easier to juggle the roles now. I might have climbed even higher if I hadn't stopped work during the baby stage, but I'm glad I did. My children are the most creative part of me. But once I did go back to work, combining career with their care was as much as I could manage. I experienced a severe attack of meeting-itis. My church commitment suffered. I was there every Sunday – and it was a lifeline – but I had little to give back in return. We can probably do two out of three well: church and work, church and children, or work and children, but the third, which will be different at different phases of our lives, will always be the poor relation. And when do the domestic chores get done?

It was hard to admit I couldn't be a domestic diva. Peter and I were both totally committed to hospitality, but some strange law seemed to dictate that as my professional skills grew, my home-making skills declined. We had to rejig our lives. I left all the financial accounting and DIY to him, because I was useless at it, and he left the cooking to me, because he hated it so much. We learned slowly and painfully to share the childcare and the chores.

'I've cleaned the floor for you,' he said one night.

'No!' I shouted in exasperation. 'You haven't done it for me, you've done it for us. This is *our* home.'

Sometimes his ministry and work took priority, some-times mine – but stopping to spend time together was essential. My Jewish upbringing taught me the impor-tance of the family meal, especially on a Friday night. It's too easy to dismiss Sabbath because our society has rejected the idea, yet this is one of the Ten Command-ments, not to stop our fun, but to make sure we have it. If God modelled it, the least we can do is follow his example. It's not about sabbatarianism – establishing an ascetic set of rules about what we are or are not allowed to do. It's about creating breathing space for God, for relationships, for us. It was the only time when we had extended prayer together round the meal table. It was where our children learned to intercede for the world.

Women can help bring a sense of reality to the workplace – and that means some must go for the top jobs. Too many of us doubt our own ability to get there. Apparently, men see the 75 per cent in a job advert they can do and go for it, while women tend to see the 25 per cent they can't and hold back. Or is it that women weigh up the consequences of career promotion against their relationships and feel the sacrifice is just too great? But it need not be. Someone has to challenge the crazy culture of the workplace and put their leisure first. Someone has to say, 'Time to go home.'

Most companies talk about their staff needing a good work/life balance. Doing it is another matter. Not taking adequate time off is a Protestant cultural attitude and is totally unbiblical. The Jews had three pilgrim festivals a year, all lasting eight days. It took two days to walk to Jerusalem from Galilee and two days back – that adds up to about six weeks' holiday a year, without all the other many essential one- and two-day festivals. And Jesus celebrated them all. Yet the Victorian industrialists, Christians as many of them were, thought themselves generous if they gave their workers two days off a year. How easy to be incredibly blind to basic God-given principles.

What will all those extra hours at work, beyond the call of duty, achieve for the kingdom of God? That's the key question. We can never recoup the hours of friendship, listening, learning, reading, sharing, eating together and praying, that we so often throw away on extra business meetings, so-called crises, unnecessary phone calls and those last ten emails. Oh yes, I forgot – the mortgage has to be paid. All I can say is that when Peter went to theological college and we had no income at all, it still got paid – even if our faith was tested to the limit. Losing a job is not the worst thing that can happen to a Christian. It is far worse to lose our faith, consumed by the materialistic values of a society built on a fragile economy and destructive concept of success.

Ultimately, we are called to be radical – salt and light, like the young prophet Daniel in captivity in Babylon, who adapted to the culture, sought only its good, yet refused to compromise his faith. The Babylonians thought that their Jewish captives would make lousy slaves as they insisted on one day off a week. In fact, on the other six they worked harder than everyone else and achieved so much more that it earned them respect for their faith. We are called to make the world a better place – a kingdom place. There is no greater privilege.

God at Work

Irene's Story

I walked fast, hardly daring to believe they would be there again. Suddenly, I saw them, exactly where they had been the day before. Relief flooded through me and then I had a new thought: would Bonnie remember me? I slid onto the park bench opposite and looked up hesitantly. Bonnie immediately caught my eye and smiled. I sighed, reassured, and settled back to listen.

As soon as the group had finished their church outreach 'routine', they began mingling with the crowd that had gathered to watch. Bonnie made a beeline for me and introduced me to Gena, who was with her. 'Remember I told you about her yesterday?' she asked me.

'Of course,' I said, looking at Gena with interest. I was still mystified by the sudden change in Bonnie's expression the day before when I had told her my name. 'Do you think you could come back tomorrow?' she had asked, after a pause. 'There's someone I think you should meet!' So here I was, hoping that now all would be revealed.

Gena suggested we go straight to the drop-in café that served the outreach. As soon as we sat down, she showed me a diary entry from six weeks before. I was amazed to see my name written there with a short comment beside it: 'Pray for Irene, she's looking for me but she doesn't know where to find me!'

I gasped as I remembered that six weeks before, I had been travelling to north Wales to attend an aikido summer school, complete with afternoon seminars delivered by a Buddhist monk. A horribly mangled marriage had left me coping with two very hurt children and suffering from unspeakably black depressions, and I was searching desperately for some kind of answer to the mess my life had become. I remember standing with a Bible in one hand and my aikido sword in the other and saying to whoever was out there, 'Show me!'

Before I could say anything, however, Gena flicked the pages over to two weeks later. There again I saw my name with yet another comment beside it: 'Keep praying for Irene, she's coming. . .'

I'm not quite sure what happened at that moment, but I had a sudden sensation of the floor shifting away from me. I found myself standing, very small and insignificant, at the end of a vast row of huge, stately pillars, arranged in pairs down a seemingly endless corridor. And then I heard a voice, indescribably tender and full of gentle invitation, speak from the distance: 'Irene!' Time stopped and the sound seemed to hang in the air, suspended as it were in some eternal space where it had always been and always would be. In fact, I can still hear it in my head even now, as clear as it was then.

It's difficult to describe the experience without making it sound either weird or overstated, but I know that was the moment I met God. I was overwhelmed by the knowledge that he knew me by name and had called me to be his. How could I resist? Even now, telling the story 26 years later, I can again feel the tears stinging my eyes and the same breathless, almost heart-stopping sensation in my chest: God loves me personally and called me by name.

This may seem like an unusually dramatic introduction to our Lord Jesus Christ and his wonderful salvation, but I was a very sinful and damaged individual at the time. God's clear call has held me steady through the many storms and struggles that have ensued since then. If your call is less dramatic, it is no less real, for God works with us each individually and does exactly what seems best to him.

These are the words of promise God spoke to his people, Israel, when they rebelled against him and were violently exiled from their homeland. They are also true for us as New Testament believers:

> But now, this is what the Lord says –
> he who created you, O Jacob,
> he who formed you, O Israel:

> 'Fear not, for I have redeemed you;
>> I have summoned you by name; you are mine.'
>
>> (Isaiah 43:1)

A little later, God tells his people that one day he will bring them back to their land because his love is even more faithful than that of a mother:

> Can a mother forget the baby at her breast
>> and have no compassion on the child she has borne?
> Though she may forget,
>> I will not forget you!
> See, I have engraved you on the palms of my hands. . .
>
>> (Isaiah 49:15–16a)

'O the deep, deep love of Jesus, vast, unmeasured, boundless, free! Rolling like a mighty ocean in its fullness over me.' So say the words of the old hymn (by S. Trevor Francis, 1834–1925). Jesus has carved our names into his hands in his own blood, even when we were still sinners and hostile towards him. What confidence we have, what assurance, knowing that the Father 'chose us in him before the creation of the world' (Ephesians 1:4).

Let me end with the words of my favourite hymn:

> Before the throne of God above, I have a strong, a perfect plea,
> A great High Priest whose name is Love who ever lives and pleads for me.
> My name is graven on His hands, my name is written on His heart!
> I know that while in Heaven He stands no tongue can bid me thence depart.

When Satan tempts me to despair and tells me of the
    guilt within,
Upward I look and see Him there who made an end of all
    my sin.
Because the sinless Saviour died, my sinful soul is
    counted free,
For God the Just is satisfied to look on Him and pardon
    me.

Behold Him there, the risen Lamb, my perfect, spotless
    Righteousness,
The great unchangeable I Am, King of glory and of grace!
One with Himself, I cannot die, my soul is purchased by
    His blood,
My life is hid with Christ on high, with Christ my Saviour
    and my God.

(Charitie Lees Bancroft, 1863)

5: Travelling in Excess

Diane-Louise Jordan

In his book *Traveling Light* (Nelson Thomas, 2001) Max Lucado describes in spectacular detail his inability to travel without unnecessary clutter.

Well, my confession is that I totally identify with this talent, because I am the 'Travelling in Excess Expert' – despite many years of travelling with *Blue Peter*, *Songs of Praise* and other television programmes. I take all sorts . . . just in case!

Perhaps my most successful trip, excess-wise, was to Bangladesh. I'm very proud of that achievement. I was part of a team assigned to film a Water Aid project and I took bottles (no, let's be honest, crates) of my own water just in case! My logic went something like this: if I'm going to an area where I *know* the water's scarce, it only makes sense to take my own – even if the film being made is about the celebration of a new well that provides safe and healthy water. . .

So as not to be caught out in any eventuality, on this particular trip I surpassed myself. I'm sure I took everything, including fresh ground coffee, fruit, biscuits, salad, nuts, pasta, peanut butter, Marmite, cheese, wholemeal bread, muesli, chocolate, bottled water, kettle, hot water bottle, wet wipes, sheets – there was nothing I didn't have! We were staying in the middle of nowhere and I've had too much experience of excessively long filming days where there is no time to take a food break, or on the rare occasions when there is time, no cafés or Costa Coffees on hand!

Please don't be lulled into thinking this is just a consequence of foreign filming. A few months back I was filming in Portsmouth, in the south of England. On the first day we began work at 7.30 a.m. and finished at 12.30 at night, with just a 40-minute mid-morning break where the only thing consumed was coffee and cake. Now this is hardly enough food for a slip of a girl, let alone a burly film crew lugging heavy kit around for nearly 17 hours. By early evening hunger had taken its grip on the normally good-humoured crew, and it was hardly surprising that they were uncharacteristically tetchy. Unfortunately, on this occasion yours truly, in an effort to travel light, didn't have any supplies. . .

In Bangladesh, despite initial jibes from my colleagues about my huge suitcase full of just-in-case emergency supplies (which happened to be bigger than me – not hard, I know – and heavier than the crew's equipment), everyone was delighted to share my fresh coffee, cheese rolls and fresh fruit at our regular 3.30 a.m. calls.

But hope is on the horizon, because recently there have

WORTH KNOWING

been a few occasions when I have managed to 'overnight' with just a small holdall. However, if the excess of my suitcase represents my life, it's evident that I still have too many heavy loads to shed. Yet unlike the contents of my suitcase, which on occasions have been a blessing, some of the loads I carry – and sometimes cling on to – I know God wants me to drop.

One of those loads is the burden of shame that sadly too many of us carry. Why are so many of us plagued by it? And what's the difference between guilt and shame? Harold Kushner, in *How Good Do We Have to Be* (Back Bay Books, 1997), says, 'We tend to use the words guilt and shame more or less interchangeably, as synonyms for feeling bad about ourselves.'

But psychologists and anthropologists see them as separate emotions. Basically, they see guilt as feeling bad for what we have done or not done. Guilt, say the psychologists, is a judgement we pass on ourselves. It's a voice inside our heads telling us we've done something wrong. Shame is feeling bad for who we are, measured against some standard of perfection or acceptability.

In his book *Mere Christianity* (HarperCollins, 1952), C. S. Lewis suggests that we all have an inherent knowledge of good and evil, and he bases his entire case for Christianity on what he believes is our instinctive moral code, our natural or basic understanding of right and wrong. When we do wrong our conscience is alerted. Our guilt makes us feel uncomfortable for a reason, it makes us aware of our sin, and it has been this way since the beginning of time. It was a feeling of guilt that made Adam and Eve hide from God.

The worst thing we can do is try to hide our guilt and not respond to it, to bury it so deep we become immune to its calling – allowing it to rob us of the joy God intends for us. Denying genuine guilt can have terrifying consequences. At his trial, cult leader and ritual killer Charles Manson was asked before sentencing if he had anything to say. Pointing to the jury, he seethed, 'You have no right to try me! I did what I felt was right!'

Unlike guilt, a judgement we pass on ourselves, shame is a sense of being judged by others. It's not just an inner voice, but a sense of being exposed, being looked at and judged by others whose opinions we take seriously. Shame is the product of a community. And it can overshadow us in so many ways.

Shame can overshadow us if we have asked for forgiveness but can't forgive ourselves, or accept that we have been forgiven. It can overshadow us if our faith is dominated by subjective feelings, rather than trust in what Scripture tells us about our having been forgiven. And shame can cripple us if we feel 'tarred with the same brush' – the shame of association, most frequently associated with family. Radio 4's *The Archers* has an ongoing storyline that illustrates this well.

Susan Carter, an intensely moral and respected member of the Ambridge community, lives under the shadow of what's known as the 'Horrobin Inheritance' – the ignominy of being unfortunate enough to be born into the Horrobin family, notorious for constantly being on the wrong side of the law. Although she now has her own family and is unquestionably trusted, she feels tarnished by association. Indeed, she had a spell in prison herself, not because she initiated any wrongdoing, but because she was faced with the painful decision of sheltering her fugitive brother or revealing his whereabouts to the police. She reluctantly chose family loyalty and paid the price. More recently Susan's daughter embarrassed the family and Susan regarded that situation as a failure that yet again pointed to her personally.

Susan Carter feels bad about herself because she is connected to a family she believes doesn't measure up to a standard of acceptability. She feels exposed and judged by others because of the action of those near to her. As a consequence shame is embedded in the *person* of Susan. Of course, Susan Carter is a fictional character, but her storyline mirrors the way so many of us live our lives. Her character is trapped by a shame that we know all too well.

Shame can also overwhelm us if we've been raised on a poor emotional diet, constantly being told that we're no good. It is said that if a child lives with encouragement, she learns confidence. If a child lives with acceptance and friendship, she learns to give love to the world.

What others say about us has a profound impact on how we see ourselves, especially what is spoken over us in our formative years. If we are fed a diet of praise, we are likely to feel good. Unfortunately, too many of us have been raised on a poor emotional diet that has led to too many of us feeling bad about ourselves. Well-known Christian speaker Joyce Meyer is convinced that 85 per cent of our problems stem from the way we feel about ourselves.

A few years ago I was invited to speak at a well-known young people's event. My subject was self-worth and identity, something close to my heart. I began the session with this question: 'Hands up – who thinks I'm gorgeous?'

Being either very truthful (!), or deluded, or just lovely warm young people, most of the hands in the room shot up and saved me much embarrassment.

Then I asked the next question: 'Hands up – who thinks themselves beautiful?'

Very few hands were raised. I remember how sad I felt that so few were able to acknowledge their own beauty.

Ironically, a few years later, I was challenged by this very question in a profound way. Generally, since becoming a Christian, I've had a reasonably healthy self-image, but at this particular time I was struggling to believe I was OK, let alone gorgeous. You see, God had been prompting me to look a little closer and more honestly at myself.

This digging deeper compelled me to look at aspects of shame in my life, aspects that had been with me for so long they'd become a part of my nature. I was hit with the realisation that I had learned to live with a deep-rooted shame. But God had been nudging me to face it. You see, he wants us released from shame, because Jesus came to set the captives free. Shame keeps us captive. Shame was stopping me from receiving the full grace and blessing of the Father.

Joyce Meyer says, 'One of the saddest things that can happen to a child of God is to have so much available and yet never be able to enjoy any of it.'

Because of his grace, even when bound by shame we enjoy some of what is available, but we could enjoy so much more if we were totally released from bondage. So what can we do to eliminate shame from our lives?

Jesus wants to bring out our best, to rid us of shame, to free us totally from condemnation. God really does transform lives – this is the true miracle. When people say, 'It would take a miracle to change,' they're right! And this is the type of miracle that only comes from God.

He died to give us *life* and give it to us in abundance. We must start knowing and believing this.

The way he wants us to receive this 'best' is for us to ask him for the courage to put him first, no matter what. To draw closer to him through his Word, not just through feelings (which can be unreliable), but 'in Spirit and in Truth' – truth being the Word of God.

We are already free, we are not captives. He wants us to believe him and not the lies of the Accuser.

When we acknowledge our shame:

> He is faithful and just and will forgive us our sins and purify us from all unrighteousness.
>
> (1 John 1:9)

> As far as the east is from the west, so far has he removed our transgressions from us.
>
> (Psalm 103:12)

> Therefore, there is now no condemnation for those who are in Christ Jesus.
>
> (Romans 8:1)

This is the truth.

Jesus' action on the cross removed our blame, our sin. And his desire is to sing over us:

> The LORD your God is with you,
>   he is mighty to save.
> He will take great delight in you,

> he will quiet you with his love,
> he will rejoice over you with singing.
>
> (Zephaniah 3:17)

Maybe you've had enough of being held back by shame, the lie that imprisons us. Why not take this opportunity to meditate on the lyrics of the following song and allow God to convince you of his love.

Blameless

The day will come when this world you've made will surely pass away
I'll be blameless on that day
In that dark hour your act of love took my guilt away
I'll be blameless on that day

I will stand before the Lord while saints and angels sing
Lost in wonder, lifted up, I'll glorify the King
Free for all eternity the past now has no hold on me
Thank you for this word of grace you say
I'll be blameless on that day

'It is finished,' was the cry that took my shame away
I'll be blameless on that day
The gift of life you gave to me took your life away
I'll be blameless on that day

(Nick Herbert/John Peters, 'Blameless',
Survivor Records, 2004)

6: Living Without Regrets

Fiona Castle

'If you were to die today, what are the things for which you would be remembered?'

I don't think I would have the courage to ask my family for the answer to such a question – but if they spoke at my funeral, they might be sensitive enough to mention the good bits and leave the rest alone! It's a challenge, because we all know characteristics of ourselves that we hope others don't notice.

What steps could we take today to make a difference? Steps that would prevent us from saying at the end of our lives, 'What if. . .?' or, 'If only. . .' It's said that the second half of a person's life is made up of the habits she acquired in the first half. How true! Sometimes it's good to stand back and take stock of our lives in order to see if we are where God wants us to be, doing what God wants us to be doing.

If memories and experiences of our lives were compared to rocks collected in our backpacks – surely guilt and regret would be among the heaviest of them – regret tends to be sorrow over the consequences of our decisions, both the sinful and the simply unfortunate. God promises to remove the guilt of those who seek forgiveness, but does not prevent the consequences of our sin.

(*Touchpoint* illustration, 'Regrets', NLT)

Life changed dramatically for me when my husband died. That seems an obvious statement. I had to learn to become a single woman again; I had to face the tears and sadness of bereavement; I had to take on the work of two people, after 31 years of a shared workload. These were all predictable and I knew that by God's grace I would cope. I'd had two and a half years to prepare for such a possibility, since the day he had been diagnosed with terminal cancer.

The unexpected change happened the day after my husband died. I was phoned by the chief executive of the charity then called Cause for Hope Appeal and told I was to be on GMTV on Monday. This was Saturday! 'But don't worry,' she said, 'I'll come and stay with you tomorrow night and take you up to the studios in the morning and make sure you're all right.' With that, she rang off and left me, openmouthed, panicking and terrified. Me? On GMTV? That's not what I do! That had been my husband's job, not mine. Many times I had waved him goodbye, saying I'd be watching him and hoping he'd get it right. But me? I couldn't do that. I was stunned. I did the only thing I could think of doing at such a time – I prayed. 'God,' I said, 'I can't do this. You know I stammer and can't get my words out. I might say the wrong thing. I'll make a mess of it. I'm sure this is not what you want me to do.'

The answer came immediately and almost audibly: 'Rise to the challenge.'

'But God,' I protested, 'suppose I fail?'

'Then you won't be asked again,' came his logical reply.

It was then that it dawned on me that so much of my fear was based on pride. What would my friends say? Would they laugh at me for making a fool of myself? Rising to the challenge would mean leaving my comfort zone and taking risks. Another thought hit me. One day I was going to have to stand before God and answer him. 'Where were you when I needed you? I gave you all these opportunities and you didn't take them. You could have made a difference.' This was a life-changing revelation. How much better it would be to try and fail than just not to bother.

I was reminded of a time many years ago, when I was about to embark on my rather inauspicious career in show business. My father took me on one side and in a very special father–daughter moment encouraged me to make the most of every opportunity and not to be afraid of doing things I wanted to do. 'I lacked courage to do some of the things I really wanted to do, and now I regret those unmet challenges,' he confessed. I thanked him for being so honest, although I was silently astounded at such a confession, for I never imagined he lacked courage for anything. He had served in the First World War and he was a wonderful doctor, much loved by his patients, faithfully serving them, charging them little and sometimes nothing if he knew that times were hard. I kept these words at the back of my mind as I went through the various stages of my life, but they burst into reality again after this revelation.

I am sure there is no one who goes through life without regrets of one sort or another – regrets about doing things we wish we hadn't and not doing things we wish we had, whether in our behaviour, our attitudes or our choices. We have the choice of allowing those regrets to prevent us from laying the past to rest, or moving forward with determination to make the most of whatever days are left to us. My favourite definition of success is a person who gets up again and gets going one more time than he has fallen. If the Lord is the focus of our dreams and challenges, then we are secure, even if we fail, because he is the inspiration to rise to each challenge he sets before us.

Some years ago I heard a sermon about 'Purpose'. The comment that stuck in my memory was that we have to go through the 'process' in order to get to the 'purpose'. This might seem rather a vague statement, but the illustration was that Jesus went through 30 years of 'process' in order to have three years of purpose. Sometimes we feel as if all we are doing is meaningless and fruitless. But we have to retain our integrity in all we do, so that our record is untarnished by the time we reach our purpose. We might think we are just treading water, but actually we are swimming towards our goal and we must always trust that God has our purpose in view.

There is a testimony of a man who all through his young life felt that God was calling him to the mission field. His dream eventually became a reality when God sent him, with the blessing of his church, to some far-flung part of the world. After just one year, God said to him, 'That's it! You have fulfilled your mission here, now go home!' Can you imagine how he felt? He was totally deflated. How would he tell his friends back home? They would think he was a complete failure. It took a lot of courage to face the music back home. But his obedience bore fruit, because he subsequently became one of the most trusted and valuable teachers of mission, in a Bible college in England. He retained his integrity through his obedience to God, whatever criticisms might have been thrown at him.

On a television programme shortly before he died, my husband was asked by Alan Titchmarsh, 'What was your finest hour?' His answer was interesting: 'I think my finest hour is yet to come. I think it will be the last hour I am *compos mentis*. If at that moment I can look back on my life and smile . . . that will be my finest hour.'

Every time you break a moral principle, it becomes harder, not easier, to act with integrity. Everything you have done in the past, including things you have neglected to do, comes to a head when you are under pressure. That is why developing and maintaining integrity requires constant vigilance and discipline.

> Do not do anything you would not want to read about in tomorrow's newspaper.
>
> (Bob Gass on UCB's *Word for Today*)

This is consistent with thinking of life as a process. If we act with integrity in all the day-to-day decisions and plans we make, we don't live with the fear of skeletons being discovered in the cupboard.

It is important to recognise that every person has a different purpose, because God has given each of us different opportunities, gifts and places to be. The temptation is to compare ourselves with others who seem to be doing more or appear to be more successful, or perhaps have fewer disasters than we do. 'It's all right for them, but what about me? I'm insignificant, I have no influence, I'm only *me*!' Perhaps, if we are in the upper age group, we are tempted to think, 'It's too late, I'm too old. I'll leave it to the younger ones!' But we might have grandchildren, and we have responsibilities to make sure the world is a little better because we have been in it.

- What can we do to make a difference?
- Do we take a responsible attitude towards the environment?
- Do we help those in the developing world?
- Can we be a voice for the voiceless, the persecuted and the hungry?
- Do we make sure that our influence on those around us reflects the love of Jesus?

God loves to use things we think are insignificant, if we are willing to offer what we have to God. I sometimes think that God cares more about our availability than our success. As Tony Campolo writes in *Christianity* magazine, 'God doesn't call the equipped, he equips the called.'

How available are we? I would like to think that I can say, 'Here I am, wholly available,' as the Chris Bowater song states (Springtide/Word Music, 1981), but perhaps I'd be more honest if I sang, 'Here I am, fairly available'!

A few years ago, I was chatting with God about the work I had been doing and I said, 'God, you don't need me to go abroad any more, do you? I've done my fair share of travelling and there's plenty of work for me to do in this country, and besides, I'm getting on a bit!' Less than an hour later, Ron Newby – founder of the charity Global Care (of which I am a patron) – phoned. He told me he was intending to make a video in various different countries where the charity worked, so that the sponsors of the children and supporters of the projects knew that their money really was making a difference. I agreed that it was a good idea, then he told me that he wanted me to front the video and it would involve going to Romania, Thailand, Calcutta and Sri Lanka – all before Christmas! After I put the phone down, I said to God, 'OK, I get the message!' If by making that video I could make life better for even one child, I had no right to sit in my armchair. I suppose we are all in danger of selective hearing at times.

I have been deeply challenged by John Ortberg's book, *If You Want to Walk on Water, You've Got to Get Out of the Boat* (Zondervan, 2003), showing us that in order not to end our lives with remorse and regrets we have to be willing to be like Peter. Unlike the other disciples, he left the safety of the boat and stepped onto the waves to walk towards Jesus. It was only when he saw the size of the waves and realised his inadequacy that he began to sink. But at least he got out of the boat with a spirit of adventure. He knew that wonderful moment of water-walking which the others missed by staying within the safety of the boat. Jesus says:

If you try to keep your life for yourself you will lose it, but if you give up your life for me you will find true life – and how do you benefit if you gain the whole world, but forfeit your own soul in the process?

(Luke 9:24–25, NLT)

Are you willing?

God at Work

Debs' Story

On the 23rd November 2003 I woke up broken. Broken face, broken hips, broken insides, broken voice. I don't think I did anything to deserve it, but that's what happened. A car crash: head on. My friend in the seat next to me. Both of us broken.

About two weeks before the crash I had a picture. I had reached a point where I had to admit that my 'life' life and my 'God' life were not intersecting, and I was desperate to see what to do. I was stuck. Life had gone well for me in many ways. I had worked hard and had amazing opportunities; had stayed in third-world hovels and millionaire mansions; studied with the best minds at university; and cleaned up after the very poorest scraps of humanity. I had filled two passports by the time I was 18. I had presented and produced television programmes. I had written and directed theatre, documentary and short film. I had the world at my feet, but it wasn't working. God wasn't working for me, and I couldn't deal with it. So two weeks earlier, I had been on my knees saying, 'I don't care what it costs, please show me how this works.' And I saw a picture of broken glass. Lots of pieces of beautiful blue glass, shattered on the ground. There was a light source above, but a reflection was coming from only one piece. I felt God say to me, 'That's your life.' And it was right. My life: many pieces, only one reflecting him.

I woke up in hospital to the growing realisation that I might never walk, or talk, or look beautiful again. My independence, my ingenuity, my value. And although the first few days in intensive care were a curious bubble of amazing peace – knowing that people were praying and feeling totally safe, when the sedation started to wear off and realisation hit home, I got really mad at God.

'Why did I trust you? Why did I listen to you? Who's going to want me like this?'

And his answer came: 'Am I more than enough for you now?'

'I don't know. Let's see.'

For the first week or so, people encouraged me not to look at my face. I knew it had been badly lacerated in the accident, and they were expecting some paralysis as facial nerves had probably been severed. But I went along with it and didn't look – only seeing the reactions in the eyes of my friends and family as they came to visit. The first time I saw my reflection was in the lift on the way up to the ward from High Dependency. Most people wouldn't notice, but when you're flat on your back a reflective ceiling brings whole new possibilities. I was pretty shocked. The whole left-hand side of my face was an angry red with an ugly z-shaped scar going from my left ear to near my nose, then down my cheek, then back across my chin. It was all still pretty swollen, which didn't help. Kind of Jabba the Hutt meets Freddie Kruger. Not what you want, really.

After the initial shock and tears, I felt quite pragmatic about it. Obviously my life will be different, I thought, but that's OK. I'll play a different part from now on. I don't need people. I'll be the scar-faced girl. I won't expect anything, so I won't get hurt. I can do that.

I never truly knew what it was like to be loved until that time. I thought people loved you because of what you gave them. A straight exchange. And because I now had nothing to offer, I thought they would have nothing to give. I didn't understand why people kept coming to sit with me – to read me stories, bring letters and pictures, watch movies. I didn't understand why a boy I had met only days before the crash kept coming back to visit. Why didn't he run in the opposite direction? I didn't understand why we kept getting messages from around the country, around the world, saying that people were praying for us, and loving us, and holding us up to God. Now I do understand: it's unearnable; it's part of the precious privilege and mystery of being a human loved by God.

And God. See, I always knew that he loved me, but I didn't really know what that meant – and I think I was worried that he didn't really think of me that much. Not enough to do anything special with me. So I always took care of that myself. I asked him for help when I thought he might want to, but I always chased after the things that I thought would make me special. I did it for myself.

So when one of my sisters arrived back from overseas a month or so later, a new Christian and totally besotted with the Bible and God's promises, and asked if we were praying for healing, I found myself not totally able to answer. I realised I had been so focused on getting through the days, on surviving, that I hadn't really thought about what would happen if I prayed. And there was my sister, talking about praying for my face to be healed, and my legs, and my voice. Suddenly I realised that I really didn't know if I could do that. I didn't know if *he* would do that. I knew he could, I just didn't know if he would.

Alone in the ward that night, I thought long and hard about it. All the reasons why I shouldn't put my hope in him. Why he might not deliver. I so desperately didn't want to be disappointed. And then a thought dropped into my head: 'What do you know about me? Who do you know that I am?'

I thought about the things from the Bible that I knew: 'You're the Deliverer. The Healer. Provider. Saviour. Restorer of Broken Places. You are More Than Enough.'

WORTH KNOWING

He said, 'Yes. So let me be me. Don't worry about what it looks like. Just give me room to be me in your life – you won't be disappointed.'

So that's where we started from: no control, but believing that I wouldn't be disappointed. There were so many incredible moments – actual miracles, with my body, with other people, sometimes just with me and him. Sometimes I felt as if I'd been plucked out of my life for a love-fest so that I would finally understand. Sometimes it was terrifying, and sometimes boring. Sometimes it was just a huge relief.

After ten weeks of traction and total dependency, I was discharged from hospital. Three months later, I'd had enough of not being able to speak, prayed with some friends, and my voice got unparalysed overnight. About a month after that, following intensive physio and rehabilitation and a bleak report from the doctors saying I wouldn't be able to walk without crutches, my mum had had enough, prayed for my legs, they straightened out instantly, and I was walking within the week. Also, I don't hate my face. The nerve ends weren't severed, and the scars which were so angry at the beginning are barely visible now. Most amazing was the boy who kept coming to visit. A year to the day from the crash was our wedding day – excessive make-up not necessary.

Before we got engaged, but after I was walking and talking again, I was at a women's event at my church and someone gave a picture from the stage. It was of pieces of broken glass on the floor, every one of them reflecting the light at a different angle, in a different direction.

I nearly lost my breath. When the crash happened, I assumed that the broken pieces would be put together again: that God would mend the glass magically, so it could reflect him properly. What I hadn't realised was that he's not remotely worried about it all looking correct and unbroken. He's not waiting for my scars to fade, or my limp to go, or my voice to work, or the man to propose. He's waiting for every area to reflect the light. So deceptively simple. Broken glass reflecting the light. Beautifully, unutterably, irrepeatably unique. And totally safe in his hands.

7: Can't Stop that Lovin' Feeling

Annie Kirke and Minu Westlake

Every woman has a relationship story which is incredibly personal, sensitive and unique. It can range from the lofty heights of friendships, falling in love, dating and negotiating physical boundaries, marriage and children, to the painful lows of singleness, unrequited love, abusive relationships, rejection, stepping over physical boundaries, getting hurt, divorce and the inability to have children. It's very rare to meet a woman for whom the relationship game has been plain sailing. Most of us will have faced highs and lows in relationships and tasted the bittersweet cocktail of floating on air one day and the next day hoping to fall asleep and wake up with amnesia!

Being single in your 20s, 30s and beyond is hard. Finding a Christian guy when the odds are so bad is a challenge. Not having sex outside marriage is tough. Staying pure and working out what that really means is confusing. Watching your friends constantly getting together with guys, going to another wedding without a special someone, and feeling ready to have children but without the prospect of marriage is painful. Lying in bed in the stillness of the night and asking God, 'What about me?' and hearing your words echo back to you in the spiritual airwaves can be faith-destroying.

Perhaps the worst part is that we start to question God's intention towards us. If we're honest, we begin to question his love for us and whether in fact he is purposefully withholding happiness from us so as to teach us the hard lesson of relying and trusting him completely.

Let's start at the very beginning

There is an eternal quest deep in the hearts of men and women to be loved and to love. To be loved unconditionally by a love so powerful and so strong that our hearts are restless until they find this love, and to respond in love with every bit of ourselves – our heart, our mind, our soul and our strength.

We feel it so acutely that there is no doubt that it is real – it propels us consciously and unconsciously to find it. In the same way that physical hunger can only be satisfied by food, our heartfelt hunger can only be completely satisfied by the love and life for which it was originally created. This love and life is God. God *is* love and he is the Creator of life. The love quest in the heart of every man and woman leads to the heart of God. We are his beloved and we were made to love him with every bit of ourselves.

We could say that God's creation of man and woman is the greatest love story ever. Spielberg's work is amateur next to God's epic story. This story is a page-turner. Not only did God create us to love and be loved by him, but also to enjoy loving human relationships, the most personal of which is that between man and woman.

We were created for committed, intimate relationships

The story of the creation of the first man and the first woman is powerful and insightful. It illustrates clearly that God created men and women for committed, intimate relationships. In Genesis 2 God created the man and the Garden of Eden, in which he set the man to work and bring order. But man was alone, which God said was not good, and he decided to make a suitable 'helper' (v. 18). So God put Adam to sleep and created Eve to be his 'helper', or *ezer kenegdo* in the original Hebrew. For years, the identity and role of women has been disfigured by the incorrect translation of *ezer kenegdo*. The NIV translates it as 'helper' to Adam, painting a subservient role for the woman in relation to the man. Theologians agree that this is a defective translation of who Eve was created to be. The Hebrew word *ezer* means 'one who surrounds, protects, aids, helps, supports'. David uses the word *ezer* in the Psalms when he says, 'The Lord is my Helper.' Eve was created to be powerful, mighty, a source of help, support and protection. She was not a sidekick. In fact, if Eve had been described solely as Adam's *ezer*, then that would have suggested she was more powerful than him, but the Bible says that she was his *ezer kenegdo*, and *kenegdo* means 'one who is the same as another', meaning that God made Eve to be an equal to Adam.

> For this reason a man will leave his father and mother and be united to his wife, and they will become one flesh.
>
> (Genesis 2:24)

Right from the beginning God intended men and women to come together in a relationship which was mutually exclusive and recognised as such by their family, friends and community. We call this exclusive, public commitment 'marriage' and in the intimacy of this relationship, God intended men and women to have sex and 'become one flesh'. For God, sex outside marriage is a no-no. It is a sin. Why? As theologian Crispin Fletcher Louis says, 'to have sex with someone outside of marriage is actually self annihilation'. This sounds ridiculous, but think about it. Think about the commitment men and women make in their wedding vows:

> To have and to hold, from this day forward, for better, for worse, for richer, for poorer, in sickness or in health, to love and to cherish 'til death do us part. And hereto I pledge you my faithfulness.

God created sex to be the most intimate way human beings give themselves to one another and he intends it to be part of a total commitment exclusively between two people for all of their lives. To have sex without the covenant of marriage is to desire the physical union without any other level of commitment to that person. Ultimately this is the desire to gratify one's own sexual desires by *taking* from another person, rather than the desire to find fulfilment in *giving* oneself to the other person. It really is self-annihilation, which is ultimately what happens to us whenever we choose to sin – we die spiritually.

The truth is, God loves sex. He created us for it and so it follows that our desire for it is good, but without the boundaries marriage creates, we end up abusing each other and ourselves.

Sex, power and authority

In Genesis 1:28 the Bible says that when God created the man and the woman he gave them two commands: to populate the earth, that is, to have sex, and to subdue the earth, which meant asserting their God-given authority and power to extend order into the surrounding chaos. This was God's amazing plan for us as his children – to create life ourselves, and to bring order to chaos on earth. However, in Genesis 3:1–19, men and women chose deliberately to disobey God for the first time in their lives, and it had catastrophic consequences. In separating themselves from his love, their identity and purpose became corrupted. Sex, power and authority became confused and men and women got hurt. We're still getting hurt. The confusion permeates relationships right across society, resulting in hurtful behaviour and painful consequences.

Our culture maintains that true sexual freedom lies in an individual's right to satisfy her sexual desires whenever, with whomever and wherever she wants. The Bible teaches the opposite, that our bodies are in fact temples of the living God and we have been made to be holy and pure, physically as well as spiritually:

Or didn't you realize that your body is a sacred place, the place of the Holy Spirit? Don't you see that you can't live however you please, squandering what God paid such a high price for? The physical part of you is not some piece of property belonging to the spiritual part of you.

(1 Corinthians 6:19, *The Message*)

Our sexual purity is an intrinsic part of our relationship with Jesus, because it affects our thoughts, emotions and actions. Jesus stresses this in his teaching in the Sermon on the Mount:

But don't think you've preserved your virtue simply by staying out of bed. Your *heart* can be corrupted by lust even quicker than your *body*. Those leering looks you think nobody notices – they also corrupt.

(Matthew 5:28, *The Message*)

Can't stop that lovin' feeling

Jesus knows that when we are tempted to sleep with our boyfriends or to mess around with guys sexually (and that means any sexual activity), our decision to do it is always influenced by what is already going on in our head and our heart. When we allow lustful thoughts to consume us, they easily begin to dictate our decisions and behaviour. Take a moment to think about some of the ways you can protect your mind – perhaps you love those cheeky romance novels which are 'just a bit of fun', or you regularly like to lose yourself in a chick flick (sometimes the same one repeatedly), or you have to buy certain magazines which focus on 'finding your dream guy, keeping your dream guy, and marrying your dream guy in ten weeks!' What thoughts do they plant in your head? How

WORTH KNOWING

do they make you feel about yourself, relationships and sex? Are they helping you to stay grounded in the truth of who God has made you to be, what he says about relationships and what he says about sex? If not, then maybe it's time to ditch them for a dose of God-reality. A recent survey of Christian and non-Christian women revealed that 66 per cent of non-Christian women masturbated, and 66 per cent of Christian women did too! This proves that we are all grappling with the issue of fantasy and it cannot be divorced from our desire to pursue sexual purity.

Guilty as charged!

Have you ever noticed that no matter how much you might not want to sin, you sometimes feel powerless to stop yourself? You're not alone. Paul says it well in Romans 7 when he writes:

> But I need something *more*! For if I know the law but still can't keep it, and if the power of sin within me keeps sabotaging my best intentions, I obviously need help! I realize that I don't have what it takes. I can will it, but I can't *do* it. I decide to do good, but I don't *really* do it; I decide not to do bad, but then I do it anyway. My decisions, such as they are, don't result in actions. Something has gone wrong deep within me and gets the better of me every time.

> (Romans 7:17–20, *The Message*)

Sexual temptation is normal if you are human and have a pulse! Jesus was tempted in every way, therefore he was tempted sexually too, so he understands and can help us to resist it. Often the church has been the least gracious and forgiving place to share our sexual struggles and admit our mistakes, as if they are somehow worse than other sins. But the truth is that to Jesus all sin is sin – it's *all* bad for us! He just wants to forgive us, cleanse us and set us free to live again. Check this out:

> Who would dare even to point a finger? The One who died for us – who was raised to life for us! – is in the presence of God at this very moment sticking up for us. Do you think anyone is going to be able to drive a wedge between us and Christ's love for us? There is no way! Not trouble, not hard times, not hatred, not hunger, not homelessness, not bullying threats, not backstabbing, not even the worst sins listed in Scripture . . . None of this fazes us because Jesus loves us. I'm absolutely convinced that nothing – nothing living or dead, angelic or demonic, today or tomorrow, high or low, thinkable or unthinkable – absolutely *nothing* can get between us and God's love because of the way that Jesus our Master has embraced us.

> (Romans 8:34–39, *The Message*)

Sharing the journey

There is power in sharing your personal relationship story with Christian friends who know you and love you and whom you trust. As secrets, fears and hidden shame come out from the darkness into the light, they lose their power over us and we can begin to know the freedom that God longs for us to enjoy. Here in brief are three personal stories. We hope they will inspire you to share your story with some of your friends.

Suzie

When I was ten or eleven my parents separated. It was a very traumatic time and home was a constant battleground. I had a lot of money thrown at me – I was spoilt

WORTH KNOWING

and wanted for nothing materially – but the one thing I really wanted was love shown through touch and time and words of affirmation. I was the ugly one at school. I didn't look like a girl, I felt rejected at times by other girls because I had short hair and no front teeth, and when at ten I became the 'tall geek with breasts', things didn't feel any better. But things did start to change. After a run of a few teenage relationships, I met my first love at the age of 14. He was 18: tall, very sexy and such good fun to be around. The mess at home made me realise I had such a hole inside that needed filling, and he seemed the perfect fit.

I found myself getting drunk and pushing physical boundaries because I wanted my boyfriend to love me. I knew in my heart that sex and love were intertwined and so I thought that this intimacy would ultimately lead to marriage and the security that I was longing for.

At 15 I lost my virginity, and I'll be honest: the sex was great. We'd discussed the future; we planned to get married once I'd left school. But I became unhappy in the relationship. I started to grow up, but he didn't! Meantime, the ache inside me for real love became more obvious and painful. I'd been to church when I was younger and I started to think more about God. I started to think about the fact I'd actually had sex before I was married and I started to regret some of the choices I'd made.

I ended the relationship right in the middle of being diagnosed with depression. I was very unhappy, feeling lonely and unloved. I lay in bed one night and said to God, 'If you're real and you want me, then show me you're there, don't let me get any worse, give me a sign.'

Two days later someone from a church knocked on the door. I knew that was God and I began going to a course to explore Christianity. During this time I continued to search for love and marriage from men. I went from one relationship to the next. At 18 I got involved with a charity and agreed to work at a Christian weekend for them. It was the first time I felt as if I knew what I'd been missing. It was God. Everyone just looked different to me. They had problems and struggles, of course, but they also had God. That weekend I became a Christian.

My life didn't change overnight. I continued getting into relationships with non-Christians, mainly because I thought Christian men wouldn't want to be with me because of the mistakes I'd made; and I continued to go too far physically in these relationships. At 21 I decided I would no longer continue in non-Christian relationships, and I would not have sex again until I was married. It was a hard decision to make, but a good one.

I've had lots of prayer, talked through my past with some older Christian women, and now, four years later, I do feel free of the guilt and shame of my past, but I'm living with the consequences of the choices I made by ignoring what the Bible teaches us about sex and relationships. I know what it feels like to feel the shame when it hits. I know what the pain feels like when you give someone that gift of your body and then they become an 'ex'. I know the look in boys' eyes when you tell them you're not a virgin, and it's then that I realise that I made a choice for which God has forgiven me, but where the consequences can carry on for years.

Annie

I'm 31 and have been single for nine years, and by that I mean I have dated a few guys, got really close to a couple of guys and ended up having 'the conversation', which I'm sure only Christians have, about whether we're supposed to take things further, and in both cases, prayed about it and felt that we weren't! That was painful on both sides, but I knew I had to respect the fact that God seemed to be saying no. So it's been nine years of not going out with anyone and not snogging!

I became a Christian when I was 16 and I was a really shy teenager, especially around boys. So when I went to university I was in no rush to get into a relationship with anyone, but happy just getting to know them and finding out how they ticked. In my first couple of years at uni I went out with two non-Christian guys, as most of the Christian guys I met were geeks and I wasn't interested! At the start of those relationships, I made it really clear where my physical boundaries were, and very quickly they became frustrated that I wouldn't let things go further, which became a real tension between us. I hated it because I couldn't trust either guy not to go too far, and I would know that I would have to be the one who was always slamming on the brakes when we spent time alone. It felt really lonely and it was this tension that split both relationships up. In both cases I went further than I wanted to physically and compromised my boundaries and desire to stay pure in my relationship with God. I had to ask God to forgive me and heal the wounds I had incurred through it, which he did.

Although I do know girls who have gone out with non-Christian guys who have totally respected their boundaries, they have been the rarity, and so following these two experiences I decided to kiss goodbye to dating non-Christians and wait to meet a Christian bloke. Miraculously, I met a really cool Christian guy about a year later and we started going out. But to my dismay, he was just as confused about physical boundaries as the previous guys! This threw me, because I had presumed that we would be on the same page when it came to pursuing holiness physically in a relationship, and so I came out of that relationship thinking, 'Have I got this all wrong? Is it me? Is everyone else reading the Bible differently from me?' But in chatting to other people I was assured that it was right to desire to be pure, right to want to please God with our bodies, and that sexual purity is an essential part of what it means to be in relationship with God wholeheartedly and to honour the other person as yourself. So when that relationship ended, I realised that I had quite a lot to learn about relationships and so I said to God that I wouldn't get into another relationship until I felt him tell me to go for it – which, nine years later, is perhaps a dangerous prayer to pray!

So what have the last nine years been like? To be honest, at first I wasn't worried at all, because I was young, there was loads of time, and I imagined that it would just happen when I was least expecting it. I hardly prayed about it at all. But as time marched on, it started to feel wrong. Some of this came out of the true desire in each of us that comes from having been made for marriage, but some of it came from an expectation that I had a right to get married. I had somehow superimposed my list of 'rights' onto God and was living with a false idea of what he should and shouldn't do in my life. God used it to begin stripping away my false ideas about him and about whether I was choosing to put my hope and trust in him for my life. It's amazing how much of Eden has been confused by Hollywood!

In Hebrews 3 and 4, Paul writes about how in the desert the Israelites were constantly swinging from trusting God to provide for them, to doubting and disobeying him. As a result, they didn't enter the resting place God had promised them. I know that in the area of relationships I could easily swing between trust and disobedience and miss God's 'resting place', the place where my heart is soft, open and expectant. The key is prayer. However, I found that praying about relationships over a long period of time could start to drive me crazy inside, leaving me feeling more anxious about it. These verses in Philippians 4:6–7 really helped me to understand that I could experience freedom in the waiting and trust in God for the outcome:

> Do not be anxious about anything, but in everything, by prayer and petition, with thanksgiving, present your requests to God. And the peace of God, which transcends all understanding, will guard your hearts and your minds in Christ Jesus.

I've also found that I couldn't have stayed sane over the last nine years without amazing friends, family and Christian community. Sharing my life with people who love me and whom I love too helps prevent sadness, loneliness and isolation creeping in. Unhealthy or sinful lifestyle habits are less likely to develop because we are accountable to others. Staying in community helps protect us from developing hard edges and keeps our hearts soft, pliable and open to meeting new guys and potential relationships.

I've got a few friends who have given up waiting for a Christian guy and started dating non-Christians. Most of them got tired of waiting and felt angry with God for not answering their heart's desire, and I understand that pain. The impact has been that, with only one exception, they have all started sleeping with these guys and have also pulled back from their relationship with God.

I know that if I wanted to I could go out and meet a guy today, I could flirt and lead him on. But I'd know that it wasn't what God wanted for me, and so I have a choice. I am compelled by God's love for me to wait expectantly for all that he has for me each day. This might mean I get married, and it might mean I don't. Only he knows – and I trust him.

Minu

I got married in my early 30s, having reached a point of feeling content with my singleness and not knowing whether I would or wouldn't get married. After being married for a couple of years, my husband and I found out that we couldn't have children and we went to everybody to get prayer. If a person moved, we asked them to pray! We were so persistent – just like the persistent widow in the Bible; we desperately wanted God to answer our prayers. God did an amazing miracle in our lives and we do have a wonderful daughter, but God did not answer our prayers in the way that we expected him to.

This whole experience made me realise just how much I had expected to be able to have children when I was married. Talking with other women, I soon realised that this expectation was not only held by me, but by nearly all of us. It had never entered our heads that this life event could turn out differently. In many ways it is easy to see how we make these assumptions. The majority of us grow up and enter adulthood with a set of expectations about how our lives should unfold, believing we have rights to certain life events occurring. It's not until they are not fulfilled that we are faced with the realisation of how much we define ourselves – and others – by them. If we, as women, find we do not get married or cannot have children, does this become what defines us as a woman? And if so, does this mean that we aren't 'a complete woman'? Of course not, but we can so easily believe the lie.

We can be prone to come to God with our expectations and present them to him as if he is some cosmic slot machine in which we put in our prayers and he delivers the goods. Jesus never promised that he would do that. He said that we should take up our cross and follow him. Some of the disciples gave up everything to follow Jesus – including their lives – and as Christians we are called to do the same. For all of us, taking up our cross means laying down our expectation that God will give us the 'perfect' life, in exchange for the promise that if we'll follow him we will experience true life and live it to the full.

So maybe you can think about your expectations – for relationships, marriage, children, life – and consider whether they are steeped in God-reality. How will you view yourself if these expectations do not become reality?

How will it affect your view of God and his love for you? How will it affect your love for him? Ask yourself what defines you: is it God, or is it something else?

Please remember:

- If you are single, it is not the only truth about you.
- If you've had sex outside marriage, it is not the only truth about you.
- Not being able to have children is not the only truth about me.

Why not pause today, and ask God to reveal afresh his truth about you and how *he* sees you?

8: Women of Worship

Vicky Beeching

Have you ever sat in a café or on a bus, and heard someone humming part of a song? You leave and carry on with your day, but suddenly you find you're humming that same tune. That happens to me all the time! It's a small example of the way that the people around us influence our lives. I read a quote recently by the writer Miguel Cervantes which relates to this: 'Tell me what company you keep and I'll tell you what you are.' It's so true – we are influenced and shaped by the people we spend time with. The Bible also emphasises this in Proverbs: 'Whoever walks with the wise will become wise; whoever walks with fools will suffer harm' (Proverbs 13:20, NLT).

I really want to spend time with people who will help me become more like Jesus. One way I do this is by looking at the inspiring people described in the pages of the Bible. As a woman, I especially like looking to the 'girls of God' in Scripture for advice on how to live. Over the years, they have become my role models and mentors in living the God-life. I love reading about them and hope some of their godliness will rub off on me! I see these women as 'travelling companions' on life's journey. I want to walk alongside them, spend time in their company and become more like them.

One particular area in which I want to be inspired is worship. As a worshipper and a worship leader, I love spending time with people who pass on to me their contagious heart of love for God. I have spent some time getting to know the women in the Bible whose hearts were filled with worship, and whose lives inspire me to praise God. Hopefully you will find their stories an inspiration on your own journey of worship.

These women are not just distant, inspiring figures. They are our family members; our sisters in Christ. They experienced what it means to be a daughter of God and know his Fatherhood. They were also human, just like us. I don't want to portray them as flawlessly superspiritual women, or we might feel guilty and unable to measure up. The reason why we can learn from them is that they had pain, struggles and weaknesses just like us.

They had a deep awareness of God's work in their lives. As we remember his mercy, his song rises up within us. Zephaniah says:

> Sing, O Daughter of Zion;
>   shout aloud. . .
> Be glad and rejoice with all your heart,
>   O Daughter of Jerusalem!. . .
> The LORD has taken away your punishment,
>   he has turned back your enemy.

> The LORD, the King of Israel, is with you;
>   never again will you fear any harm. . .
> The LORD your God is with you,
>   he is mighty to save.
>
> (3:14–17a)

They also had another secret: they had learned to hear God's song of love over them. That is the greatest way to increase your heart of worship – hearing and experiencing God's love for us. As 1 John 4:19 says, 'We love because he first loved us.' I hope you not only hear the songs these women offer to God, but also the song of love that God sings over you:

> He will take great delight in you,
>   he will quiet you with his love,
>   he will rejoice over you with singing.
>
> (Zephaniah 3:17)

Have you ever run a marathon? I wouldn't dream of trying to compete, but I enjoy watching them on the television. Often I wonder if some runners will finish, as they look so discouraged and exhausted. I've noticed that often they look to the crowd for encouraging faces and supportive words. Sometimes it seems that the support of the onlookers is what gets them to the finish line. The Bible gives us a similar picture in Hebrews:

> Since we are surrounded by such a great cloud of witnesses, let us throw off everything that hinders and the sin that so easily entangles, and let us run with perseverance the race marked out for us.
>
> (Hebrews 12:1)

If you feel discouraged or even just in need of some refreshing in your worship, look to the women in the following pages. They are standing at the edges of the race track, and calling us to persevere in praising, trusting and loving God.

One of my favourite quotes is from the writer and philosopher Søren Kierkegaard. He once said, 'A friend is someone who knows the song in your heart and can sing it back to you when you have forgotten the words.' Perhaps you are overflowing with praise for God, and have never felt more excited about him. Perhaps you are experiencing a dry and difficult time, and need a fresh reminder of his grace. If the song of love in your heart has grown faint, I pray that these biblical women will sing it back to you and remind you how it goes. May they encourage us all to sing it louder and stronger in the days ahead. . .

Miriam

Miriam is one of my favourite women in the Bible. She seems to be the first female worship leader we see in Scripture, so she is one of my heroines and inspirations! The sister of Moses, she experienced God parting the Red Sea and rescuing Israel from their Egyptian enemies. The full story is found in Exodus 14. Once the Israelites were safely on the other side of the waters, Moses overflowed with a song of praise to God. Next, Miriam stepped forward to lead the people in worship:

> Then Miriam the prophetess, Aaron's sister, took a tambourine in her hand, and all the women followed her, with tambourines and dancing. Miriam sang to them:
>
> > 'Sing to the LORD,
> >   for he is highly exalted.

The horse and its rider
he has hurled into the sea.'
(Exodus 15:20–21 *NIV*)

Watching her in this cameo 'movie scene', I feel she has much to teach us. First, Moses' and Miriam's songs following one another are a beautiful picture of God using both men and women in worship. Male and female have an equal and unique role, and something precious to bring in their offering of praise.

Sometimes we see others serving and contributing and might feel like sitting back and just watching, even though we feel God's prompting to step out and lead. Miriam is a good role model in this: although Moses had just led the people in song, she knew she also had contributions to bring. So she took a deep breath and rose up to glorify God. If God is encouraging you to step out as a worshipper or a worship leader, remember that he has made you unique and can do unique things through you as you obey his call.

I love the way Miriam took what she had at that moment – her tambourine and her voice – and used them in worship. (OK, so tambourines are in need of a serious image overhaul these days! But in today's culture that might be a piano, a guitar, your voice, your creative skills of art or dance. . .) Sometimes we postpone serving or leading because we don't feel qualified. Miriam just took what she already had, and used that as her offering. This reminds me that as a worshipper I just bring what I have and who I am at that moment, and turn it into praise. Sometimes it's joy, at other times it's tears from a broken heart. Sometimes it's well rehearsed songs, and at other times it's spontaneous and unpolished music . . . but whichever it is, she tells us simply to start with what and who we are.

Miriam was a woman who had been through a great deal. She grew up amid the harsh slavery and persecution of her people. She watched as Pharaoh worked them to the bone and murdered their children. It was a long season of pain and seemingly unanswered prayers. However, after God brought Israel to safety, she didn't look back on the suffering with bitterness. She praised God and thanked him for his deliverance. She challenges us to choose to worship, in both good and painful times.

There's a snapshot of Miriam. We could linger with her much longer, but our next guest is waiting. Let's head over and sit awhile with Hannah. . .

Hannah

Hannah's story is found in 1 Samuel 1 – 2:11. If I'm ever in need of a reminder that God welcomes real and honest worship, I open up 1 Samuel and hang out with Hannah for a while. She knew pain and suffering as intimate companions, as she was unable to have children. In her culture that was an extremely shameful burden to bear. Not only was she barren, but those around her mocked her harshly and caused her many tearful nights.

In 1:10 we see her response to barrenness and other people's cruelty: she takes it all to the feet of her Father God. It says she was deeply distressed and prayed to the Lord weeping bitterly. What do we do when our hearts are breaking and we can't stop the tears from falling? Do we run to God's embrace? Hannah reminds me that when I

WORTH KNOWING

am falling apart, I shouldn't run away from God, but straight into his arms.

Her honesty and expression of sadness before God was so strong that the priest thought she was drunk. Sometimes, as a fairly reserved person, I struggle with expressing emotion. I need encouragement to be fully open in expressing my heart to God in worship, and Hannah shows us that God welcomes us to be totally real about our hurt and sorrow in his presence. She inspires me to be fully honest and vulnerable when I draw near to meet with God.

Hannah also shows us the role of sacrifice within worship. When God answered her prayers and sent her a son, she gave him back to the Lord, to live and serve in the temple. In 1:24–28 we read about her giving her son to God as an act of gratitude. I want to offer God a sacrifice in my worship; to bring him all of me, and all that is precious to me, and fully surrender it to him daily.

Hannah knows how it feels to have a broken heart. She shows us what it means to bring God honest worship and a deep sacrifice of thanksgiving. Next, let's grab a cup of tea with Deborah and hear her breathtaking memories about life on the front lines of the battlefield. . .

Deborah

If an award was to be given for an Old Testament woman 'with guts', Deborah would probably win it hands down! Her story is found in Judges 4, where the passage describes her as 'a judge', 'a prophetess' and a 'wife'.

In a time when Israel was in trouble – in danger from their enemies and needing someone to rise up and be a strong leader – Deborah said 'yes' to God's call. She was such a reliable and comforting presence that the commander of the army said, as he prepared to take out the troops to war, 'If you go with me, I will go; but if you don't go with me, I won't go' (Judges 4:8). So she went beyond the call of duty, accompanying the army into battle and enabling them to win a great victory.

In the busyness of our lives, it's helpful to see role models of women who juggle lots of roles and tasks, yet live lives of worship and faithfulness to God. She inspires me to say yes to God's call, whatever he asks. She encourages us to go beyond the call of duty, and do all we can to help and serve God's people. Her wisdom is also amazing – Israel must have been hugely strengthened to have her counsel and understanding. Proverbs says that we should seek out wisdom like treasure and greatly desire it. Seeing how much Deborah's wisdom helped Israel is an inspiration to pursue wisdom and ask God for the ability to advise others well.

When they had won the victory, I love the fact that her response was to sing! The people of Israel said to her, 'Wake up, wake up, Deborah! . . . Break out in song!' (Judges 5:12). The whole of Judges 5 is subtitled 'The Song of Deborah'. Her response to God's goodness and deliverance was instantly to pour out her heart in song.

If you are feeling overwhelmed by busyness or too many roles to juggle, or feeling afraid at something God is calling you to step out into, take some time to hang out with Deborah in Judges 4 and 5. She will encourage you, and she is an awesome role model worshipper to cheer us all on!

Our next friend is standing in the back corner of the room. Out of all these women she is probably the least familiar. She is the 'Beloved' from the Old Testament book Song of Songs, or Song of Solomon.

Beloved

This woman is the leading lady within Song of Songs. The book is a love story – it could be a Hollywood romance! – about falling in love and praising the beauty of the one you adore. The book shows the worth and greatness of human love, and it also echoes the love relationship between Christ and his Bride, the church.

The Beloved in the book can teach us much about intimacy within worship. If you read the story from the perspective of God loving and pursuing his people, you see how much he treasures and values us. We also see how intimate and heartfelt were the exchanges between the Beloved and her lover, and it encourages us to unveil our hearts to the Lord when we worship.

Intimacy is often a scary thing. I've heard the word 'intimacy' explained as 'into-me-he-sees' (which I thought was pretty clever wordplay). It's scary and uncomfortable to have the depths of your heart and soul seen by another. Sometimes we approach God in worship and feel the need to cover up our brokenness or hold back part of our heart for fear of being let down. The Beloved in this book reminds me that we can allow God to see the depths of who we are, and that there is no need to be afraid.

As the story progresses, we see the Beloved becoming more and more bold in her words of love. The more she receives his words of affirmation, the more free she feels to express her love in return. I mentioned 1 John 4:19 at the start of this chapter: 'We love because he first loved us.' If we want to become more loving worshippers, then we must first soak in his words of affirmation to us. As we said earlier, Zephaniah 3 describes God singing over us and celebrating his love for us with dancing. I want to have this reality soak into my soul. The more it does, the more love for God rises up within my heart in worship.

If you have time, go through Song of Songs and see the ways in which the Lover pours out his affection for his Beloved. Some of it beautifully describes what God wants to communicate to our hearts. Here are a few to get us started.

You are so beautiful my beloved, so perfect in every part.

(4:7)

How beautiful you are my beloved, how beautiful.

(1:15)

Let me see you, let me hear your voice. For your voice is pleasant and you are lovely.

(2:14)

You have ravished my heart, my treasure, my Bride, I am overcome by one glance of your eyes . . . How sweet is your love.

(4:9–10, NLT)

Let's receive God's tender love for us, and in return unveil our hearts and bring him intimate and heartfelt worship. Someone who really understood how to do that was. . .

Mary of Bethany

Out of all these women, Mary of Bethany would have to be my favourite. She models worship in such a visual and powerful way – in fact, Jesus said that wherever the gospel is preached, her act of praise would be remembered. She has much to teach us.

If you haven't read about her, check out Mark 14:1–9. Jesus was sitting at dinner with friends when Mary entered the room, took a jar of perfume and broke it over his feet. It was recorded in the Gospels and stands as a powerful moment in worship history.

The first way it inspires me is through a desire to be an 'extravagant' worshipper. Her perfume cost a whole year's wages – an annual salary. Now that's a serious amount of cash! She went above and beyond, to thank Jesus for his love and forgiveness. I want to live a life of giving God my highest and most precious sacrifice, and when I worship I want to sing and pour out my heart, holding nothing back.

Mary also models great bravery. She could have given the gift to Jesus in private, but she chose to walk in uninvited to a dinner party with many eyes watching her. If I ever feel afraid to praise God in front of others on stage, I remember her courage.

The Gospels tell us that some in the dining room reacted negatively to Mary coming in and 'wasting' the perfume on Jesus' feet. She shows me that even when others might be hostile, we should not lose heart and should continue to worship and serve Jesus wholeheartedly. I have been part of some worship gatherings on the streets, and sometimes passers-by are rude and critical. In moments like those I cast my mind back to Mary and take heart from her bold, courageous example. May it inspire us all to be more extravagant and unafraid in our worship!

Over to you. . .

We have spent time in the company of some amazing women in the last few pages: Miriam, Hannah, Deborah, the Song of Songs' Beloved and Mary of Bethany. I hope they have encouraged your heart – they certainly have inspired mine.

Don't just leave it there. The Scriptures are filled with characters who have much to teach us about worship. Find them and let their stories fire your heart to praise our awesome God!

God at Work

Jean's Story

I was at Waverley Abbey, at a Christian conference weekend. I was a new Christian, having come to faith at the age of 35, and was very hungry for more of God. Being a divorced woman was not easy and I was now living as a single person, longing for a new husband to share my faith and my life. This particular weekend was called 'How to Live the Single Life', and I really did need the help.

At the end of the weekend we had the opportunity to take communion in the lounge and to receive prayer. At this point my room-mate got up and I thought, 'Great! She needs prayer,' as I had listened to her pouring out her problems all weekend! At that very moment my chair seemed to tip forward and I was on my feet heading for the front. I was trying to figure out who had tipped up my chair, and started to panic. But as I was on my feet, I had no choice, so I knelt at the coffee table and was immediately surrounded by people who put their hands on my head and shoulders.

Feeling awkward and embarrassed, I closed my eyes, as this was a totally new experience for me. Then the most amazing thing happened: I felt as though I was kneeling at the foot of the cross and Jesus was looking down at me, and I felt love pouring down over me and through me. It was as if I was being soaked in love and it was the most amazing experience of my life; I could have stayed there for ever.

At the end of the weekend, I drove home and said to God on the way back, 'If you can make me feel like that, who needs a husband!'

The next morning in my bathroom I looked over to the window and there was what I can only describe as a hologram of a man's head and shoulders. A voice in my head said, 'This is your husband.'

I was totally dumbfounded, but remember saying, 'He looks too young for me.'

Immediately there was a reply: 'He needs to be young to keep up with you!'

I had not recognised the man, but felt compelled by God to pray for my husband.

A few weeks later at church I was asked to be in a team investigating church-planting. In the team was a man named Jonathan, whom I'd seen but never met. To be honest, I always thought he looked a bit boring – and he obviously had no dress sense. The following Sunday at church I heard a voice in my head saying,

WORTH KNOWING

'Jonathan is nice, you'll like Jonathan.' Throughout the service God kept repeating the same thing over and over again, until I said to a friend that I needed to talk as I was being driven mad by something. 'I think God's trying to fix me up with Jonathan Lupton,' I said. My friend commented that he was not my type, and I added that for another thing he was younger than me. . .

Soon after, the church-planting group discussed a church visit – but only two people were available to make this trip, me and Jonathan. Meeting to discuss the visit, we had tea and I told him how I had become a Christian and he started to tell me his story. Looking at him, I saw the face I had seen that day in the bathroom. 'Help!' I thought. 'This is the one God said is going to be my husband, but he isn't my type!' Jonathan told me that he became a Christian at Oxford University. I went to Oxford too . . . but it rained that day! I had left school at 16 with hardly any qualifications.

The next week we headed up the A1. I suggested that we stop on the way, and as we entered a tea room Jonathan immediately ordered for us both, which quite took me aback. But as we sat down I heard God say in my head, 'Let him do it,' and at that moment, as I looked at Jonathan, I felt a wave of love go through me. When I got home I just said to God, 'OK, wrap him up, I'll take him.' But nothing seemed to happen and I felt rather unsure of what to do next.

So I decided to take things into my own hands. I phoned him and asked if he would like to come round to my home for a meal, thinking I would impress him with my cooking skills. We had a lovely evening and towards the end I started to tell him about my experiences down at Waverley Abbey and being filled with the Holy Spirit. I told him that the next morning God had given me a vision of who my husband was to be. There was silence, and then Jonathan said, 'Is there any more coffee?' After he left at the end of the evening, I told God again that Jonathan was obviously not interested. But every day God reminded me to pray for him and every time I saw a rainbow I heard the words, 'I keep my promises,' so I stuck little rainbow stickers on my phone and on mirrors. But Jonathan still didn't phone. . .

Months passed and I kept praying. I started going to another church nearer to where I lived. It was over a year since the vision, and I went down to Waverley Abbey House again for a weekend with my mum. Over coffee, a man came up and started chatting. I told him that we lived near Nottingham and he said he had a friend there. I asked how I knew him. 'Through skiing,' he said – and I soon discovered that, yes, it was Jonathan Lupton.

He then asked if I would like to join a skiing party he was organising the following March. Of course Jonathan would be in the party too. That night I said to God, 'OK, not bad going – you managed to get a man I've never met in my life, 150 miles away from home, to invite me to go on holiday with Jonathan.' On the holiday five months later we had a great time, but still nothing romantic happened. Jonathan was a much better skier than me and was off with another group most of the time. So when we returned I was devastated and told God that he had tried his best, but obviously it was just not going to happen. But the rainbows kept appearing and I kept on praying.

Some time later a reunion was held down in London for our holiday group. On the Sunday evening we went to church and somehow I knew something was going to happen there. As the service ended I stood waiting for the blessing to be given with my hands resting on the pew and noticed that Jonathan was doing the same. Then a voice in my head said, 'Hold his hand.' I said, 'No.' The request was repeated and still I said, 'No.' Then I heard God shout, 'Do it!' which made me jump. I put my hand on top of Jonathan's and felt something like 5,000 volts go through my body as the curate gave the blessing.

I fell back onto the pew and Jonathan asked if I was all right. 'I need a drink,' I said, to which he replied that they were serving coffee downstairs. I told him that coffee might not be enough, that I needed a gin and tonic as I felt so shaky! We left the church and as we journeyed along the motorway I was still shaking and didn't speak much, but felt the presence of God still with us. Jonathan then asked me about the conversation we'd had 15 months before in my home, when I told him that God had told me who my husband was going to be.

'But you didn't tell me who it was,' he said.

We reached the bar, and as we sat there I felt very nervous. If I revealed it to Jonathan and he said, 'No way,' then who had given me the vision all those months before? If it wasn't God, who was it? And where did it leave my faith?

I took a breath, and told Jonathan that the man in the vision had been him – and then I promptly burst into tears. I looked up to see him just staring at me, and saying, 'It's as if I'd known all along.'

That date was the 5th May 1991, and we were married on the 2nd May 1992.

At our wedding reception someone told me to come outside as they had something to show me. There in the sky was the most wonderful rainbow, and I heard God say, 'I keep my promises.'

9: Life in a Postmodern World

Amy Orr-Ewing

It was strange walking down a hospital corridor with a growing sense of foreboding, getting closer to the consultant's office and wondering what he would say. I was 15 years old and was having the afternoon off school to receive the results from the operation I had undergone the week before. A mole on my leg had begun to turn dark and my doctor had decided to remove it as a precaution. My mother and I entered the office together and sat down. The consultant leaned over the desk and said, 'I'm afraid it's cancer.'

Those words still echo in my head now as I write them, the shock, the fear, the bewildering emotions that rushed through my body from head to toe. He went on to explain that it was in fact a borderline case of melanoma and that they would need to do a further operation to make absolutely sure that I was in the clear. But those stark words, 'It's cancer', stayed with me. What was life all about? What was it for? Was there a purpose for my life? Was my life over?

Well, as you have probably guessed, I survived. My life was not yet over, as it seems that God had a plan for me which was to last more than 15 years. Through the experience of the cancer, I encountered a God who is near us in suffering, a God who makes his presence known. I remember lying in my bed shaking with fear and calling out to God, who then tangibly filled my bedroom and lifted the fear and blackness from my chest. As Psalm 30:1–6 says:

> I will exalt you, O Lord,
>> for you lifted me out of the depths
>> and did not let my enemies gloat over me.
> O Lord my God, I called to you for help
>> and you healed me.
> O Lord, you brought me up from the grave;
>> you spared me from going down into the pit.

I received prayer ministry to be freed from the fear of death and experienced wonderful release from that. In all the fear and worry God was near – delivering me from darkness. As I look back now I can see that his deliverance had a purpose in my life. As the writer of Hebrews puts it:

> Since the children have flesh and blood, he too shared in their humanity so that by his death he might destroy him who holds the power of death – that is, the devil – and free those who all their lives were held in slavery by their fear of death.
>
> (Hebrews 2:14–16)

It was wonderful to experience the healing and freedom, but these were not ends in themselves – God had a purpose for me. This is what life was for, this is what it was all about, it was all to please him.

In his novel *High Fidelity* Nick Hornby gives us an insight into the postmodern mind when it comes to this issue of mortality. It is so different from facing death with the help of God:

> I saw for the first time how scared I am of dying, and of other people dying, and how this fear has prevented me from doing all sorts of things, like giving up smoking (because if you take death too seriously or not seriously enough, as I have been doing up till now, then what's the point?), and thinking about my life, and especially my job, in a way that contains the future (too scary, because the future ends in death). But most of all it has prevented me from sticking with a relationship, and your life becomes dependent on that person's life, and then they die, as they are bound to do, unless there are exceptional circumstances, e.g. they are a character from a science fiction novel. Well, you're up the creek without a paddle, aren't you? It's OK if I die first, I guess, but having to die before someone else dies isn't a necessity that cheers me up much: how do I know when she's going to die? Could be run over by a bus tomorrow, as the saying goes, which means I have to throw myself under a bus today.

> (Nick Hornby, *High Fidelity*, Penguin Books, 2000, p. 247)

Having now reached the milestone of 30, I have a longing to see women entering into the fullness of God's plans for us in the midst of all the pressure and options of our postmodern society. Postmodernism describes a wide-ranging change in thinking beginning in the early twentieth century. It is a characteristically difficult term to define, but postmodernism basically criticises the idea of any absolute or unquestioned truths. Postmodernism is characterised by some of the unique features of life in our society today, including globalisation, consumerism, the breakdown of authority structures and the relativising of ideas. Some describe postmodernism as 'cynical belief, the dissolution of cause and effect, the absence of order'. But for our purposes here, one of the most intriguing aspects about postmodernism is its lack of certainty and direction. Any sense of certainty or conviction is a very suspicious thing – it reeks of intolerance and is therefore avoided by the postmodern. As David Bowie commented when being interviewed in the *Sunday Times* magazine a few years ago,

> John Lennon, Pete Townsend and I all had this same thing of rather cobbling together one's own belief system – in my case, one that changes all the time as I need to change it. Because I cannot really come to grips with absolutism. I'm fascinated by characters like Sir Thomas Moore. I think it's because it is so alien to how I seem to cope with life. I can't understand how people can be like that. They are exotic creatures to me. How do they get to that place where they know with absolute certainty what's true?

Truth, certainty, conviction are all casualties of the postmodern mind. But this is a direct attack on our status as children of God. He wants us to be secure in who we are because we belong to him. And God wants us to know what direction we are going in because he has come into our lives, transforming us and putting us on a completely new path. That isn't to say that we always know what we are meant to be doing or where we are going, but as we walk in obedience to Jesus we are totally certain that he is with us, we try to follow his footsteps and he guides us and fills in the details on the way.

This reminds me of the woman who was walking along a sandy beach. As she was admiring the view, her foot brushed against a glass bottle which she bent down to examine. On picking it up and taking the lid off, a genie rushed out and appeared before her in a magnificent robe. He said, 'I will give you one wish. Think about it carefully – anything you ask for will be granted immediately.'

The woman didn't need any time at all. She knew what she wanted in life, so without missing a beat she replied, 'I know what I would like to wish for.'

The genie nodded. 'Go ahead, then.'

So she closed her eyes, mustered all her will power and belief, and said, 'I wish I could have thin thighs.'

The genie was horrified. 'You could have had world peace, an end to poverty, a cure for Aids, and yet you chose something this selfish. No, I can't believe it. Wish again. I give you one last chance.'

The woman looked a little guilty and said, 'You're right, it was a bit selfish. OK, this time I wish for thin thighs for everyone in the world.'

Very few people in our society have certainty or conviction about the important things in life, very few have a clear sense of direction or of all the pieces fitting into one whole. This is a symptom of our postmodern society. Yet being a Christian gives us exactly what is missing. We have a relationship with God, who has a plan for our lives, who takes us by the hand and leads us as we follow him.

That sounds very simple and easy, but being led by God in our current society, where there is such a dizzying array of options, is easier said than done. We have so many alternative beliefs, lifestyle choices, morality and career expectations to navigate our way through as women. In fact, it sometimes seems that as women we want it all – we want to be attractive, to have a respected job, to be interesting, to read widely, to find a life partner, to provide for our own retirement, to get established on the housing ladder, to have children, to look after our children, to have a beautiful home, to wear flattering and fashionable clothes, to look after a wonderful garden, to keep up with friends, to be a domestic goddess when it comes to entertaining – all with locally produced organic food . . . and so it goes on. The pressure to live up to all of this comes both from the world out there – the society we are a part of – and from within ourselves.

A common perception amid all of this is that the Bible has very little to say about it. Somehow we feel deep down that the Bible doesn't really understand the dilemmas and pressures of the postmodern woman – it was written in an age when women were confined to the home and had very few prospects other than to be teenage mothers, staying at home and producing masses of children. The Bible's affirmation of such young mothers is in stark contrast with the disdain with which our society looks at them. I live in Peckham in south-east London, where we have some of the highest rates of teenage parenthood in Europe. Many of these young parents have chosen to keep their babies and as a consequence they have to work really hard from a young age to keep their heads above water. The Bible doesn't offer motherhood as the only option for young women, though. When we read it we do see women whose sole vocation is motherhood – and they are commended, but we also encounter women who suffer with the agony of infertility. We see women who have a role in the public worship of God's people (Miriam) and others who have a role in public life, leading their nation (Deborah). The main passage in the Old Testament in which a woman is held up and commended at length for her life, character and choices may surprise and encourage us. It comes at the end of the book of Proverbs:

> A wife of noble character who can find?
>   She is worth far more than rubies.
> Her husband has full confidence in her
>   and lacks nothing of value.
> She brings him good, not harm,
>   all the days of her life.
> She selects wool and flax
>   and works with eager hands.
> She is like the merchant ships,
>   bringing her food from afar.
> She gets up while it is still dark;
>   she provides food for her family
>   and portions for her servant girls.
> She considers a field and buys it;
>   out of her earnings she plants a vineyard.
>
> (Proverbs 31:10–16)

You may have noticed that this woman is hardly a typical image of the Christian woman of whom we think God approves. Where is the bit about not going out to work? Where does it tell us that we should wear dowdy, frumpy clothes? In fact, what we have here is an amazing affirmation of a high-achieving woman. The Bible characterises her as precious – she has high value. She works hard – notice all those verbs and the energy with which she is described: working, bringing, getting up early, providing. . .

She sounds like a whirlwind of activity. I remember when I first started my job as an itinerant evangelist and teacher, the surprise with which I was received at various events. If I was part of a teaching team with my male colleagues, I was often greeted as the secretary. On one occasion, after I had been speaking in a church, an older man came up at the end wanting to give his life to the Lord. His wife had been witnessing to him for years and this particular day was the breakthrough for him. His comment was, 'That was so fantastic – all my questions have melted away. I mean, I have never heard a woman speak in this way before – but that doesn't matter, it was great – it was as if you were . . . a man.' I laughed, inwardly knowing he had meant to compliment me, but it revealed something deep and often unspoken: that in many of our workplaces there is a subconscious need for us as women to prove that we really can do it. Well, the Bible doesn't hold that over us: here in Proverbs 31 we see a woman commended for her success and held up as an example.

> She sets about her work vigorously;
>> her arms are strong for her tasks.
> She sees that her trading is profitable,
>> and her lamp does not go out at night.
> In her hand she holds the distaff
>> and grasps the spindle with her fingers.
> She opens her arms to the poor
>> and extends her hands to the needy.
> When it snows, she has no fear for her household;
>> for all of them are clothed in scarlet.
>
> (Proverbs 31:17–21)

Notice her business acumen – her trading is profitable. Notice her property speculation – she considers a field.

Notice her provision for her family and her employees – she is creating work and wealth for others. She even has good arms – no bingo wings here! Yet she is more than a successful entrepreneur, she cares for the poor in her community, showing charity to those who need it. She looks after her children and cares for her husband, making sure everyone in her household has more than they need.

> She makes coverings for her bed;
>   she is clothed in fine linen and purple.
> Her husband is respected at the city gate,
>   where he takes his seat among the elders of the land.
> She makes linen garments and sells them,
>   and supplies the merchants with sashes.
> She is clothed with strength and dignity;
>   she can laugh at the days to come.
> She speaks with wisdom,
>   and faithful instruction is on her tongue.
>
> (Proverbs 31:22–26)

She even has lovely bed linen and nice clothes! This woman is able to laugh at the future rather than fearing it, she has authority in her household and is respected, she speaks wisely and is knowledgeable about the word of God, and so is able to encourage others. No wonder people look at her and call her blessed.

> She watches over the affairs of her household
>   and does not eat the bread of idleness.
> Her children arise and call her blessed;
>   her husband also, and he praises her.
>
> (Proverbs 31:27–28)

This woman works like a Trojan! The Bible is not implying that we can become like her by sitting around – hard work is involved. A few months ago a girl made a comment to me which brought this to light. I had been helping to run a community group during my maternity leave and her observation was, 'Well, you must be Superwoman – doing all of that and looking after your children.' I felt a little annoyed afterwards. We all know that Superwoman doesn't exist; the reality is that we work hard and try to do the best we can. That is what this passage is saying: this woman puts a lot in, she invests herself in those around her – at work, at home, in her community – and she is commended for this hard work. It isn't an easy option.

Now, these exacting standards may seem unachievably high: how can we ever hope to compete? But this woman is not in the Bible to make us feel bad about ourselves, but rather to affirm that women of God can be and should be women of character, vocation, passion and energy. We can look after our families well and pursue God's kingdom. We can follow our calling, whether that be a particular career path, ministry or family role, and enter into it fully with God's empowering and blessing. We can walk through suffering with our hand in the hand of God, knowing that our life has a purpose and a destiny.

Seven months ago I gave birth to twin boys. I had longed for these babies, carried them inside me for nine months, prayed for them, feared for their survival, got fat for them, even endured pain for them. But when they were placed into my arms in the hospital . . . it is impossible to find words to express the love which welled up in me for them. My boys had been entrusted to me and suddenly I had amazing hopes, dreams, plans for them. People ask, how can you feel all of that love for more than one baby? I promise you that you can. Well, God is like that with us. He calls us his children. He is an infinite being with an overwhelming and unimaginable capacity to love us. He has plans for each of us – things he wants us to accomplish, a purpose for our lives which is wonderful and beyond our wildest imaginings.

With the certainty of our salvation and our relationship with God as our foundation and starting point, we can be guided by him through the plethora of choices, options and possibilities with which this postmodern world presents us. We can be confident that Jesus will walk with us through all that life throws at us. We can be inspired to enter fully into his dreams and plans for us – knowing that it won't be a walk in the park, but it will be fulfilling beyond our wildest dreams.

10: Designed by God

Rachel Hughes

Therefore, I urge you, brothers and sisters, in view of God's mercy, to offer your bodies as a living sacrifice, holy and pleasing to God – this is true worship. Do not conform to the pattern of this world, but be transformed by the renewing of your mind. Then you will be able to test and approve what God's will is – his good, pleasing and perfect will.

(Romans 12:1–2, NIV)

I don't think I know one woman who would say that she is 100 per cent happy with her body. There always seem to be certain lumps or bumps that we would love to change. I recently read that 92 per cent of young women 'dislike' their appearance. But we were not only 'designed' by God, but also made in his image. It must break his heart when a disgust or dissatisfaction with the gift he has given us leads to drastic measures like extreme dieting, major cosmetic surgery, and even self-harm.

We all know how common it is to feel bad about the way we look, and to feel that relentless desire to take action. We're not talking about a tiny minority of women who struggle with this issue: having a negative view of our body is as common as the magazines that exacerbate it. But by holding onto this view, we are neither living in the freedom that we're promised by God as Christians, nor choosing to worship him with the entirety of our being. So how can we stand in the face of the familiar and learn to accept, even celebrate, what we've been given, and in turn worship our Creator God?

Worshipping: 'Offer your bodies as a living sacrifice. . .'

It is not a new thought that worshipping God extends far beyond singing songs. In this verse from Romans, Paul strongly encourages us to sacrifice ourselves before God. Not literally to lay ourselves on the altar, but to surrender everything that we are to God, and by doing so, truly worshipping. Interestingly, Paul uses the word 'body' to express this idea of giving everything to God. Paul isn't saying that we *only* need to worship God with our body, but speaks of our whole being as the combination of our mind, heart, desires and, yes, our body too.

Learning how to worship God is always our starting point. It's our *raison d'etre*: to please and praise God through all that we are and in everything that we do. We need to look much further than mere participation on a Sunday; in this setting it's easy to use our body to express worship. But how we view and treat (or indeed mistreat) our body for the rest of the week is of great interest to God. When it comes to worship, it's all too easy to try to

WORTH KNOWING

separate our mind from our body, but what goes on in the mind has significant implications for what we do with our body. The two are intrinsically linked. We need to allow God access to all areas if we want to learn to truly worship him.

Although Paul is referring to our whole being in this verse, his choice of the word 'body' is striking – particularly to a twenty-first-century female reader. I can grasp more easily the concept of worshipping God with my heart and my mind, even if at times I fail to do so, but I am particularly challenged by the concept of worshipping God with my body. Of all the areas we are called to offer in worship, our body image can often be the hardest. Simply accepting our bodies as they are and treating them well can, for many of us, be the costly first step towards true worship. When I read these verses from Romans today, I'm profoundly challenged that if I don't learn to worship him through the way I treat my body, then I'm not truly worshipping.

Thinking: 'But be transformed by the renewing of your mind. . .'

It is virtually impossible to convince yourself to think differently about the way you look, and no amount of dieting, fake tan or surgery is going to change what is at the root of this destructive feeling. I'm a firm believer in effective counselling, but the very first step is always to ask the Holy Spirit to come and renew our mind. Without the mind onside, the body doesn't stand a chance. The Holy Spirit can provide that essential starting point we need to break what can often be the habit of a lifetime. But it doesn't stop there. We then need to pursue God's truth and turn away from the things that we know drag us down.

From the age of 12, I was acutely aware of my 'lacking' when it came to good looks. Combined with a growing awareness of my peers and some insensitive words from certain friends and family members, I realised that I just didn't make the grade on the aesthetics front. I was painfully skinny with hundreds of freckles, buck-teeth, a flat chest and an unfortunately prominent nose. What started off as adolescent awkwardness developed into a deep loathing towards the way I looked. Every time I looked in the mirror my reflection would disappoint me, letting me down like an unfaithful friend. I felt ugly, unchosen and unlovable. I was judged by the girls and rejected by the boys. And all the while I kept God at arm's length.

A few years later, my body had developed, I'd discovered make-up, and I'd learned how to dress for maximum impact. I started to receive the male attention that I'd desired for so long, and their superficial, hormone-driven interest seemed to be exactly what I needed. But behind the make-up and the clothes I was hurting as deeply as ever. My sense of self-worth was virtually non-existent.

I was a Christian at the time, but I hadn't invested in my relationship with God. I wasn't exposing myself to the transforming presence of the Holy Spirit or the truth of God's word, and I'd convinced myself that worshipping God could be confined to church. I was left with my own unhealthy thoughts and conclusions regarding my body image, and my mind was full of untruths about my inadequacy and unattractiveness. It was at that time that God met me powerfully. Following a prophetic word from a virtual stranger, I found myself in a crumpled, teary mess on the floor at church. I cried out all the pain while God gently spoke to me about my true worth. I felt as if my mind was being turned upside down, all the negative thoughts were being supernaturally replaced with a humble confidence that I was made 'beautiful' by Almighty God. I walked out of that church feeling like a new person.

God had transformed my mind and therefore my thoughts, which had a direct impact on the way I viewed my body. Nothing had changed externally, but I'd been given a new perspective, a new point of reference and a new identity. For so long I'd quantified my beauty against a standard that the world had set for me. Up to that point my identity had been established on how I succeeded or failed to measure up to this standard, rather than focusing on the truth of God's word. I realised that I had a responsibility to place my identity and self-worth on what God said about my body. I had a choice either to strive towards the empty and unobtainable worldly view of beauty, or to submerge myself in the word of God and find freedom in its pages.

Psalm 139 took on a whole new meaning:

> For you created my inmost being;
>> you knit me together in my mother's womb.
> I praise you because I am fearfully and wonderfully made;
>> your works are wonderful,
>> I know that full well.
> My frame was not hidden from you
>> when I was made in the secret place.

When I was woven together in the depths of the earth,
  your eyes saw my unformed body.
All the days ordained for me
  were written in your book
  before one of them came to be.

(Psalm 139:13–16, NIV)

When society told me otherwise, I clung to these words. I printed them out and stuck them by my bed. I read them relentlessly over and over and over again. I still return time and again to these verses when my self-worth takes a battering. I rely on God to fill my mind anew with his presence and truth, and I make a choice to look in the mirror and see what God sees.

I recall an innocuous yet profound conversation that I recently had with my mum. We were reminiscing about all the junk her devoted children had given her as gifts over the years: tacky mugs, dodgy earrings, hideous scarves, and the ugliest, most obscure clay pot that my brother Simon made for her when he was very young. This strange piece of pottery still holds pride of place on the windowsill in my parents' sitting room. I commented that as we had all grown up it might be time to throw away the old pot, which horrified my mum. When I questioned her desire to keep it, this was her answer: 'I won't throw it away because it speaks to me of that early spark of creativity that we saw in your brother. When you look at that pot, you see a lump of clay. When I look at it, I see Simon's hard work, I see the pleasure he got from making it, and I see the love and the thought he poured into creating it.' By the world's standards, that pot wouldn't fetch more than 50p at a car-boot sale, but to its creator (and to my mum) it's priceless.

I can't help thinking that God looks at us in a similar way. After all, we are 'fearfully and wonderfully made'. The difference being that every single inch of our body was thoughtfully designed and delicately created by the same artist who made all the beauty we see in creation. When God looks at you, he doesn't see what the world sees, he sees his masterpiece.

Speaking: ' Holy and pleasing to God. . .'

Words have power. James reinforces this view: 'With our tongues we bless God our Father; with the same tongues we curse the very men and women he made in his image' (James 3:9, *The Message*). Our words can bring life to – or shatter – others as well as ourselves. I still remember with alarming clarity the negative words spoken by others over me about the way I look. I can recall all the times I've convinced people, or my reflection, how ugly and unworthy I am, not to mention the many whispered, cruel conversations I've had with friends at the expense of another woman's looks.

I know people who simply cannot receive a compliment about the way they look. Instead of accepting it as truth, they replace it with what they think is a more accurate description. So often our sense of worth regarding our body becomes so diminished and distorted that we refuse to believe words of truth and what we see becomes inconsistent with what others see. One particular friend would ask me virtually every time she saw me whether or not she was fat. Every time I would truthfully answer her, 'No,' yet she would routinely go on to spend the next few minutes explaining in detail why my view was wrong. She was so terrified to put on just one pound of weight for fear that others would detect a difference in her shape. Her own words had begun to poison her mind, she had lost her perspective, her point of reference. Her reality had become distorted and my attempts to convince her otherwise seemed completely ineffective.

As James says, we need to learn to 'tame our tongues'. I have made a promise to a friend, preventing me from saying anything negative about the way I look when we're together. We're aware it's wrong, yet strangely our own negative words can become a comfort to us. Sometimes we don't dare believe that we are OK and this sense of striving becomes what we live for, becomes all we know.

We must keep a check on the words we speak over ourselves. Our culture will go to great lengths to persuade us that our body is not as it should be, and by accepting this lie the battle is lost. But often we not only fall victim to the words we say about ourselves, we become participants in an active and dangerous competition that sets us against each other. Why is it that even the kindest of women can relish bringing another woman down (usually behind her back) based on her appearance?

One of my closest friends is among the most beautiful people I know. My friend is kind and humble and also happens to look like a French Connection model! She's not pushy, overbearing or smug. Instead, at times, she seems almost apologetic for the looks that she has been given. I'm always intrigued by the reaction she gets when we're out together. Naturally men stare, but it's the reaction of the women that most frustrates me. They seem almost angry that someone so stunning has stepped into their space. I see their eyes searching for imperfection, something that will make them feel better about the way they look. It was only after we'd known each other for a while that she confessed to frequently feeling on the receiving end of other women's silent, angry and unprovoked jealousy.

I know I've caught myself looking at other women whom I deem to be less attractive than me, and I confess to experiencing a sense of relief at their apparent lack of beauty. In the past I've pored over celebrity magazines with friends, taking turns to assassinate verbally the person photographed by criticising their weight, their outfit, or their choice of partner. No wonder so many women have an issue with body image. And yet, as Christian women we can so easily do something about it. We can choose words that speak life and bring freedom. Words have power.

Doing: 'Do not conform to the pattern of this world. . .'

I read this in a newspaper recently:

> The fault lies with the media. Glossy magazines, for girls as well as women, collude with fashion and cosmetics firms to twist our perception of beauty. They show us airbrushed images of skeletal models – many of them mere children – to make us feel fat and inadequate, so that we will buy more products in the hope of feeling better. As a former editor of *Marie Claire* – and a former anorexic – I know how this cynical trade works; and how unhappy it makes people.
>
> (Liz Jones in the *Daily Mail*)

About 18 months ago I made a choice not to buy fashion or gossip magazines any more. I wasn't having a superspiritual moment – I had simply reached a point where I was fed up with the way those magazines made me feel. By the time I reached the last page, all I'd be thinking about was which diet I should be on, which piece of make-up I couldn't possibly go another day without, and the drastic action I needed to take about the cellulite on my thighs. I stood back and had a philosophical look at those magazines and realised that if I took away the words and images that damaged my already faltering self-image, all I was left with were adverts and celebrity gossip.

Tackling a poor self-image starts with the mind but ends in action, but taking action can fly in the face of what our culture says is OK. We need to allow the Holy Spirit to expose the root of an unhealthy body view – but we also need to undo patterns of behaviour that lead to our downfall. I knew the magazines had to go when the thought of not buying one made me panic. To this day, when I see them on sale I feel drawn, and every time I walk out of the shop without one, a small victory has been won. We must not be naive to the tactics that Satan will use to keep us trapped.

A very good friend of mine has struggled for a long time with an inaccurate view of her weight. This led to unhealthy dieting and what seemed to be the beginnings of anorexia. She would over exercise, drastically restrict certain food groups, and weigh herself every day without fail. God has been setting her free from this, and she gets more beautiful every time I see her. But in order to break free, she knew there were patterns of behaviour that had to change. The first step was to get rid of the scales; in part, it was her daily weigh-in that locked her into this destructive thought pattern. Once they were gone, something was broken.

Someone else I knew hid behind fake tan – she felt awful without it. What had started as an innocent way of looking good became an addiction. She had pinned her perception of beauty on whether or not she was wearing it. She felt irrationally OK with it on and ugly without it. Personally, I hate people seeing me without make-up. I'm terrified that they judge me as a fake for hiding what's really there with clever make-up techniques. But in order to be free, I make a point of going a day without it every so often. I feel exposed and vulnerable, and people often comment on how tired I look! But by the end of the day, I feel as if I have passed a really important test, that I can cope without it.

Of course, watching what you eat and weighing yourself isn't wrong, wearing fake tan and make-up isn't wrong, but these actions can be the catalyst for, or the symptom of, something more sinister. They can lead to, or cover up, destructive desires. It's never OK to harm our body.

Sometimes it feels as if society requires us to drag our body through dangerous dieting, cosmetic surgery or extreme exercise in order to measure up. How on earth can this be right? And how can this possibly qualify as worship to the God who made us in the first place? We need to be watchful of this subtle line. There's a big difference between losing a few pounds and starving yourself, and there's a big difference between make-up and surgery. It would be wrong to try to define where exactly this line should be drawn. Our only precaution is to seek God and to stay vigilant, ensuring that we are not buying into a dangerous and damaging lie.

Paul commands us to be countercultural, encouraging us not to opt out but to embrace what's good, and to stand against what's bad. Celebrating the body we've been given by seeking to look good is admirable. But if we stay honest with ourselves, with God and with each other, we know when this desire to look good takes on a life of its own. The focus should always be on God. This is the essence of worship, and as with everything, when this focus shifts, our worship shifts. Learning to worship God with our body encompasses our thoughts, our words and actions. It is a tragedy that so many women feel such a deep sense of failure about the way they look when God intended our different designs to be a gift. It is only when we embrace the beauty we've been given and gladly acknowledge the beauty of others that we find freedom for ourselves and can encourage others to be free. In my experience there is nothing more beautiful than a woman who knows her Creator and feels at home to worship in her own skin.

God at Work

Cheryll's Story

It began in Malaysia when I fell asleep at church on Christmas Day 1992, which was the only time my family went to church together. My mum was a Buddhist, my dad a Christian. I was eleven years old. My dad saw me asleep and said angrily to me, 'If you're going to fall asleep in church, don't bother coming.' So I rose to the challenge: after that Christmas Day, I didn't go to church for the next eleven years, apart from two occasions – my grandparents' funerals. During this time my parents began to have marital problems.

Things took a dive when I was 16. The situation at home worsened and I developed hatred towards my father for a number of reasons. I decided to open myself up to the dark side of the spiritual world, because I did not want to turn back to Christianity. I became a satanist, smoked heavily and became addicted to acts of self-harm.

I started constructing a satanic altar in my bedroom, but my sister stopped me. She was afraid I was going to sacrifice myself. My collection of satanic books grew and I searched the internet for anything connected to satanism and anyone who had a dark past. Often I had a feeling and a small voice in my heart telling me that I was capable of doing similar acts if I wanted to. It was coaching me to perform and I was tempted.

My relationships with my family and friends naturally suffered. I was under a cloud and became withdrawn from the world around me. My life had no purpose and was worthless. I battled hard with my self-worth.

At 17, I developed severe migraines and sharp pains in my heart. I started consuming high doses of painkillers. On average, I took 12 pills a day. This was also the start of my alcohol addiction. I hardly slept and I hardly went home. I was always out with my friends in bars, on the streets or at their houses till the small hours of the morning. I started to have casual sex and was addicted to pornography and masturbation. My mum became increasingly worried, but was unsure how to help.

At 18 I suffered from chronic depression and became suicidal. All my attempts failed. Looking back, I know God saved me.

One night, as I dozed off to sleep, I saw the devil's face close up and angels falling from heaven into a huge burning fire. I was afraid and knew I had gone too far, but I couldn't stop my obsession with the dark spiritual realms. I grew thirsty for it. I started to be very sensitive of the dead spirits around me; I could hear them calling me and sensed them around me. I was scared, but didn't know how to stop it all.

I was in various relationships in search of love and acceptance, but when real love came my way, I rejected it. I had built a wall around my heart so I would not be hurt by anyone. I was left numb. No emotions. I was dead.

Strangely, perhaps, despite all this, I excelled in my education and career. I suppose it was a means to prove to the world and myself that I was worth something.

This life continued until I left Malaysia for England in 2002 to complete a degree. Isolated from everything familiar, I believe God started to work in me slowly, by removing my passion or need for cigarettes, alcohol, drugs and money.

Frustrated about my state of life, on the 14th February 2004 I stood by the Thames river outside the Oxo Tower where I worked, and shouted angrily at God, 'If you're there, and you're what everyone claims you are . . . why aren't you here to help me? I am so broken. Don't you care?'

God heard my desperation and anger and sent me an 'angel'! Four days later, I started dating Paul, who is now my husband. On our third date, I found myself at a church with much reluctance. I felt I did not belong in God's home – and yet that was the beginning of my walk with Jesus.

For the first three months, I felt an uneasiness in my

heart, almost as if my heart was choked up. I felt I was the devil in the house of God, and I hated it. I wept uncontrollably during worship, I poured out all my sorrow, burdens and broken promises, crying out to God to help me. There was so much truth in the worship about God that I couldn't deny it, and I knew I had done so much wrong that all I needed was for God to love me again and forgive me.

However, I didn't know that there was such a thing called grace and mercy. This feeling was so unbearable that I often walked out of the services, but each week I kept going back to church with Paul. There was a weird attraction to it that I didn't understand. Eventually I felt my heart burning with God's love, and I decided to choose God over the devil.

Five months later, God knocked on my door when we sang 'Your Blood' ('Nothing But The Blood', Matt Redman, 2004) and I answered. I said quietly, 'God, I want to come home with you. Please accept me.' I became a Christian.

I felt my burden lifted and a great sense of peace. Through the power of Christ, I was set free. My light was burning so brightly that most friends could instantly see the difference! My view on the world and people changed. There was hope once again. It felt as if the dark clouds had passed and the sun was shining again. It was the best feeling I'd had in a long, long time. I was no longer oppressed. I was made alive by Christ.

The journey has not been smooth. It has involved lots

WORTH KNOWING

of prayer and support from my church leaders and friends. It has been a year and a half of spiritual battle, exorcism, doubt and deep healing, but all along God has shown me his grace, mercy, love, faithfulness, power and glory in each and every area of my life.

11: Keep Smiling! Dealing with Crises in Our Lives

Elke Werner

There's no way round it: crises are part and parcel of life. When I was 17, I encountered Jesus and I thought that from then on my life would be easier. But I soon realised that ups and downs would still be part of my new life with God. It's a fact. Even as Christians we still go through conflicts and crises.

As I travel around the world, I meet women whose experiences are similar to or even more difficult than mine. Over time, I realised that crises are an important part of our lives. The question is not whether we experience them, but rather how we deal with these realities.

God's camera

A little girl is playing in the garden when a storm starts to brew. Lightning strikes, thunder rolls and it starts to rain.

The girl's mother calls her to come inside. The girl starts to walk to the door, but then she stops and looks at the sky, smiles and then walks on. She stops again, looks up again, smiles again, but does not come inside. In the meantime, the girl is drenched. Still she lingers in the garden, looks at the sky and smiles. Her mother gets crosser and crosser, because the child just will not obey. When the girl finally comes into the house, her mother asks her why she did not listen. The child answers, 'I wanted to come in, Mummy, but God kept wanting to take my photo.' Every time the lightning struck, the girl thought she had to smile for 'God's camera'!

Storm clouds

Difficulties and crises brew in our lives like storms. Just when things are going well and everything seems to be coming together, along comes a crisis. Suddenly the harmony of life is disturbed and nothing remains the same. In a crisis, one area of our lives begins to dominate all others. The issue, conflict or problem edges its way in and overshadows everything else, even those areas in which things are going well. A conflict with someone, a jeopardised relationship, stress at work, arguments with the neighbours or illness dominate our thoughts, emotions and sometimes even the way we act and react.

An upsetting crisis

Let me compare a crisis with a mobile, like those that babies often have above their cots. When a mobile is knocked off balance, each individual part is knocked out of position. It usually takes time and patience to bring the

WORTH KNOWING

parts back to their original positions so that the mobile is balanced again. That's how it was with me, over 15 years ago. My husband and I were in Africa for the summer when I got very ill. It was not just the malaria or amoebic dysentery which we were used to. On returning to Germany, I was diagnosed with Hodgkin's Disease, cancer of the lymph system. Apparently the disease was already in its final stages. Given three months to live, my future as I had imagined it was turned upside down. My life now hung by a thread. In light of this very real crisis, I started to re-evaluate my entire life and tried to understand what was really important for me. Some friends pulled back, and others came closer than ever before. Our marriage proved to be strong. Roland, my husband, was a great help to me. Nobody knew whether I would live or die. My whole world was shaken.

A loss of control

What happens when a crisis hits our lives? It seems as if everything comes to a complete stop. Our everyday routine no longer works. Nothing is certain any more. Everything is put to the test. Fears and worries arise. We lose our sense of security and self-confidence and become aware of how dependent we really are. In an acute crisis, there are some who can no longer sleep, while others become depressed and take refuge in their beds. Some take comfort in eating, while others lose their appetite in the face of so much stress. Even our sense of time changes; five minutes can seem like hours, or it seems as if time is running away with us. This much is clear: in a time of crisis we can no longer cope alone. We have lost control and cannot see any way of changing the situation by our own endeavours.

A moment of decision

Our word 'crisis' comes from the Greek *krisis*, which means something like 'decision, discerning moment', or even 'judgement'. In a crisis, the situation comes to a head and a way out must be found. Things cannot stay as they are. Something has to change, adjust or improve. Such a crisis develops in every good film or play. At some point, the main character faces a decision. The outcome is not clear. The story will either end in a catastrophe, or will come to a happy end. In any case, at this moment of decision, everything is in the balance and the audience hold their breath!

Coping patterns

But what happens when we are not in the audience, but are going through the crisis ourselves? Most of us react in the ways that we learned in childhood. The example set by our parents continues to have an effect on us. Sometimes we react with activism, trying to get things moving in order to end the painful situation. At other times we react with self-pity, feeling sorry for ourselves and maybe even blaming God for allowing bad things to happen to us. Sometimes we blame any and everyone else. Anger and powerlessness are our constant companions.

A time to reconsider

Crises lay bare the ways we deal with things and show us what isn't working. They are the 'MOT' of life. They allow us to see clearly who our friends really are. They help us to evaluate our lives and set ourselves new goals. They can be opportunities to reorder our lives. What is of worth to me? What do I want to continue to do as I have done? What do I want to change from now on? In overcoming a crisis, we rethink both large and small areas of our lives. We value things in a new and different way. We see life in a new light.

Discovering God's perspective

Let's go back to the little girl in the storm. In the midst of the rain, the thunder and the lightning, she understood that she was not alone. God was with her. This realisation is the most important one we can come to in a crisis. Right where we are helpless and insecure, where we are dogged by fears and worries, God is with us. He loves us and will not leave us alone. He will not forsake or abandon us. He is there for us. This is what I understood: God is for me.

Crisis as opportunity

Crises are opportunities to grow. Several years ago, there was a scientific experiment. The goal was to create an entirely self-sufficient artificial world under a glass dome. Some of the scientists attempted to live inside that man-made world for some time. After a time, however, the experiment was aborted. Some aspects of the experiment had worked well, others had not. One of the problems seemed at first to be inexplicable: the branches on the trees in the greenhouse snapped when they bore fruit. The reason? They had not developed enough strength. Because of the lack of strong winds and storms, the trunks had not had to stand against the wind and therefore remained weak.

The insight gained from this experiment has become an example to me. Difficulties and crises in our lives serve a purpose. There will be winds and storms. But when we root ourselves in God and endure the adversities, we become strong. The psalmist expressed this insight with these words:

> Yet I am always with you;
>> you hold me by my right hand.
> You guide me with your counsel,
>> and afterwards you will take me into glory.
>
> (Psalm 73:23–24)

When we decide to hold on to God in our times of crisis, we will emerge strengthened. Our roots will go deeper with God. The tree of our life will bear fruit and not break under the weight. With the comfort God has given us, we will be able to comfort others.

Bringing God into the picture

Let me tell you what I try to do in times of crisis.

- I have learned to pray: I pour my heart out to God. I talk to him about everything. I seek his counsel.
- I have learned to talk: I confide in people who know both God and me well. Their advice can correct and direct me, so that I don't sink into self-pity.
- I have learned to reflect: I read the Scriptures and soak up God's words of promise and comfort. I learn Bible verses by heart.
- I have learned to trust: I trust that the same God who has helped me before will help me again.

Keep smiling!

Crises are moments of decision in our lives. They are opportunities to renew our priorities, to put God first and reorder our lives. Just as in a mobile the thread reaches upwards, we must reach up to God, the saving power in every crisis. St Paul puts it this way:

> Indeed, in our hearts we felt the sentence of death. But this happened that we might not rely on ourselves but on God, who raises the dead.
>
> (2 Corinthians 1:9)

When I look at my life today, I am thankful that I can still be like the little girl in the story. No matter how fierce the storm that rages around me, I know this: God sees me. God is interested in me. God loves me.

The next time you see lightning, keep smiling!

12: Just Finish It, Baby

Ali Herbert

If the music industry is anything to go by, we've got a bit of a thing about journeys. Nancy Sinatra informs us that her 'Boots Were Made For Walking', Sheryl Crow thinks 'Every Day Is A Winding Road', The Thrills are 'Just Travelling Through', Run DMC tell us in no uncertain terms to 'Walk This Way', U2 encourage us to 'Walk On', Helen Shapiro is merrily 'Walking Back To Happiness' and Canned Heat are 'On The Road Again'.

It's very natural for us to be moving 'onwards' physically, mentally and emotionally. Going backwards is never considered a good thing, and getting 'stuck in a rut' is a depressing thought. In Philippians 3:12–14, Paul says the same thing about our spiritual lives and encourages us to 'press on towards the goal' – to head towards heaven, to keep becoming more like Jesus, always to move on in our lives with God.

Sometimes our walk with God is really easy. God feels near, all our friends are desperate to know more about Jesus, we're riding on a wave of Spirit-filled inspiration, every future challenge looks exciting, relationships are blossoming and life is fulfilling in every way. Oh, it's good to be a woman of God!

Sometimes it's hard to keep going. It feels as if our prayers are hitting some kind of ceiling and bouncing down hard on our heads. Life just seems grey, and day follows day without a streak of colour or excitement.

And sometimes things get really rough, like being out at sea without a compass, tossed and turned by a storm and unsure of which way to turn next – or whether we'll ever reach land again.

Being a Christian is a lifelong journey. And frankly it's not always a smooth, rose-strewn path.

Wouldn't it be great to feel we were really confident about this journey? I'd love to be like the apostle Paul, so confident about 'running the race', about 'putting on the armour of God' (although running a race in armour could potentially be a little tricky. . .). Paul sounds as though he's always confident, always walking forward, learning and growing in the most adverse circumstances.

My husband Nick and I are quite keen on walking. We have this romantic idea of strolling through bosky dells and woodland glades as the sun sets and the bluebells twinkle at our feet. The reality is not always like that. On one of our walks we found ourselves in a large field of cows – not too unpleasant until, halfway across, Nick said in a low voice, 'It looks as if they've got *rather large* horns and they're *looking* at us.' I answered brightly, 'Nooo, it's fine!' and sped up to a power-walk, aware that Nick had a bright red jumper on. We exited the field at a random point before the large horns reached us and promptly got lost for the next three hours. On another occasion we were on our summer holiday in Northumberland – in the middle of the rainiest season they've ever had, with floods everywhere, and just after foot and mouth disease had struck the UK. We carefully checked the walks that were still permitted and set out on a nine-mile hike, only to discover, halfway round, a rather threatening skull-and-crossbones sign and some seriously glowering farmers behind it. The remainder of our 'romantic' walk was a four-mile trudge home along a busy dual carriageway in the pouring rain. Not exactly what we had in mind when we set out.

My spiritual walk is a little bit like that: not exactly what I had in mind when I first set out! I get lost, I get stopped and put off by the signs and the people I see, I get tired, I go totally the wrong way, I often walk in circles. How about you? To be honest, I think that's probably the most common experience of the Christian life – there are not many of us who are 'gloriously marching forth'. Next time you're in church, ask the people next to you if they are! Walking with Jesus – walking the Christian path – is more like taking a few faltering steps, with a couple of glances backwards and a propensity to fall over.

We believe as Christians that we're journeying towards heaven, towards being whole and perfect in Jesus. That God can see us as we will be – with every bit of our amazing potential fulfilled and even exceeded, a version of us without the hurt we carry, without the wounds that we've already picked up on the way. Don't you want to get somewhere like that?

The ancient Chinese adage says, 'The journey of a thousand miles starts with just one step.' To begin at the beginning, our first step on this spiritual path is as simple as the request: 'Jesus, please come into my life.' That's all it is. By his grace and love, it costs us nothing to take that first step.

But after that, although Jesus has done it all for us – and we can do *nothing* more to earn our place with him – the 'constraints' of love call us to move forwards. We are called to become more like Jesus, to be the person he can see and loves, to stop hurting him and 'press on to take hold of that for which Christ Jesus took hold of me' (Philippians 3:12). When I got married, I didn't see it as a done deal with no more effort to be made on my part. Nor did I think, 'Great! What an opportunity to commit adultery!' I saw a road ahead for Nick and me, with every opportunity to choose faithfulness and trust and love and commitment. A love relationship is a simple description of our journey with God. Our journey is not about what we can and can't do in legal terms; it's a fluid, living, two-way relationship where we change and mould ourselves simply because we are in love with a living and wonderful God.

But that transformation can bring a few shocks. . .

You know that moment at the end of a good night out, when you're one of the last few in that dimly lit club or candlelit restaurant, and suddenly the management switch on the lights? Horrible, isn't it? Only moments before, you were cool, sophisticated and beautiful – but suddenly you catch a glimpse of yourself in a mirror and become aware that not only have you spilled some kind of drink down your top, but your hair is sticking out at an interesting angle, your lipstick is smudged up to your nose and you have parsley in your teeth from the canapé you ate three hours ago. . .

When we step from the darkness into the light, we can suddenly see the reality. And it's not always something we like to see. The first step on our journey is full of the light and grace of Jesus, but after that we begin to see ourselves more clearly – and that's not always pretty. It's quite nice living in ignorance, but at the end of the day, if we see the reality we can sort it out and get ourselves cleaned up. We mess up on our Christian walk for all sorts of reasons – it would be very unusual if we didn't – but we have the incredible option of going to God and letting him clean us up.

As we get a bit further down the line with God, it seems sometimes that things are getting worse, that we're messing it up more, not less. But it's just that we're beginning to see more clearly in the light – and like our eyes adjusting to a bright light, it takes a little while to make the details out. When the mess becomes clear to us, we bring it to God and he forgives us. And forgets it totally. That's the Christian walk.

At this moment some of us will be seriously battling with ourselves, with living out this Christian life. Areas with which many of us will struggle are our personal relationships, our identity, our history, our sexuality, our self-worth, our money. It's hard to keep walking, to keep pressing on towards the goal when these issues constantly trip us up and turn us back on ourselves. Many of us have cried bitter tears over these things.

Much of the pain comes from words that have previously been spoken to us, or things that have been done to us. I encourage you to share your hurts with Christians you trust, and let them pray for you and walk with you as God heals you. The Holy Spirit is given to minister in deep places in our hearts, to guide us and counsel us – we need his power and healing where we are currently paralysed.

I lead the women's ministry at our church and I find that the issues crying out to be dealt with time and again are those of self-worth, sexuality and identity. The world shouts out negative and harmful messages at us every step of the way. The devil laughs as we absorb them. Instead, we must keep turning to Jesus to hear his clear voice and the truth about who we are. We can sit in front of Jesus and cry with the pain of inadequacy and worthlessness – but if we let him, he will pick us up again and again and gently set us on our way. We really need Jesus in this world.

The New Testament makes it clear that if we make a commitment to God in any way – to give money, to read the Bible, to mend or give up a relationship, to tackle our past – we're likely to get the attention of the enemy who will try to divert us. It's his job. John 10:10a says, 'The thief comes only to steal and kill and destroy.' Our job is to believe what Jesus believed and do what Jesus did. John 10:10b says, 'I have come that they may have life, and have it to the full.' Jesus wasn't put off by the enemy. We need to see an 'attack' of the enemy for what it is and move on.

Although many people are thrown off course with God when traumatic situations come their way or painful issues explode in their lives, I've found that disappointment and discouragement slow me down the most. A year or so ago, when my daughter Gracie was a small baby, I found myself feeling very much left out of church and 'spiritual' things. It wasn't really possible to go to church in the evenings and my morning church experience was reduced to sitting in the crèche and fiddling with toys that played 'Twinkle, twinkle little star' . . . endlessly. To be honest, I didn't know how I was going to get through this massive change in my life and cope with a routine that often felt mundane, exhausting and humdrum. I found I had little time for talking to God, let alone getting refreshed and standing under the 'shower' of the Holy Spirit. Then slowly I discovered that while I was breast-feeding Gracie before her bedtime, I had a really good stretch of time when she was content and quiet. We live next door to our church and on Sunday nights I could hear the congregation singing their little hearts out! I felt God say to me that his Spirit wasn't confined within that church building, and that he'd meet me right where I was – the Spirit would come and be with me as I sat in a darkened room in my rather messy house. He said to me, 'I'll speak to you there, I'll meet you there, right where you're sitting with that little baby. Even though you feel lonely and discouraged, I'm here with you – teaching you and filling you with my Spirit. You can be under the shower of the Holy Spirit right now.'

It was brilliant, and for those few months I think I had some of the best quiet times ever. God is so good. He's not just on the 'mountain top' – in the thrill of exciting ministry times and spiritual highs. He's walking alongside us wherever we are. He'll fill us with his Spirit wherever we are spiritually, physically, mentally or emotionally. We need that power to keep going on our journey, to do that most vital thing – finish well.

But walking is tiring. In Galatians it says, 'Let us not become weary in doing good' (Galatians 6:9a). So, guess what, we're not the first people to get a bit weary with this walk, we're not the first church or the first generation to find it a challenge to walk with Jesus. For 2,000 years people have found that it's hard work walking with Jesus.

The first step we take is easy – it's because of God's grace and mercy and because he's called us to join him. But from that point, it's not all marching forth of the saints, it's working out what it means to be a Christian on a rainy, cold, February Monday morning on an overcrowded tube. It's working out what it means to be a Christian when your friends are getting into stuff that you know isn't compatible with being filled with the Holy Spirit. It's tackling the past so it doesn't hold us up in the future. It's a 24-7 thing, this Christian walk, and it's *normal* to feel tired and weary sometimes – and that's OK.

When we're weary and discouraged, we need to remember that Jesus is pleased with any tentative step we take towards him. Like a good parent with a young toddler, *any* step is a delight and something to be celebrated. Gracie is just learning to take her first steps now. She's not very good at it yet – and turning corners is proving to be quite a challenge! But, you know what, it's the best thing in the world seeing those little, wobbly steps. She looks ridiculously proud of herself at every attempt, but I bet my goofy grin is three times the size of hers. I know that this is a reflection of God's heart for us. However pleased with yourself you are at a tiny step forward on your walk with him, I guarantee that he's on the edge of his seat to watch what you do and wildly applaud any tiny move forward!

We should be encouraged that this is not a journey taken in isolation. In 1 John 1:7 it says, 'If we walk in the light, as he is in the light, we have fellowship with one another.' If we're trying to walk out the Christian life, then we suddenly discover there are other people around us doing the same thing. In our generation, we have done a really good job of learning to be independent, of coping in isolation, of relying solely on ourselves – however lonely we might really be. And the church is called to subvert that, to be truly radical for our generation. That's the whole point of a church building, of the bunch of people around you. That's what the church is for: to walk with Jesus alongside each other. To encourage one another, to pray for each other and minister together in the power of the Holy Spirit. You've become part of a body. You're a 'people', a collective group, the children of God. Have a look at your fellow church members: unlikely though it may seem, you're the body of Christ!

The apostle Paul tells one group of churches not to give up meeting with each other. He knows it's vital that we encourage each other along the way. When I was younger I went to a church that nearly fell apart because of the brokenness of the people in it – lots of people left the church in dismay that other people weren't perfect and then lost their faith altogether. It's easy to think we don't need the medley of people around us, that this walk would be more pleasant if we didn't have to put up with the foibles and annoying habits of others: the bad singing voices and the peculiar religious language, the lack of humour and the wrong clothes. But we need each other. Like a coal that falls out of a fire, we quickly grow cold and the fire dies when we try to go this journey alone. I should know, I tried it myself for a while. It didn't work.

Like every Christian throughout history, none of us is perfect yet, but we walk in our brokenness together. John Wimber, the leader of the Vineyard Church movement, said we should probably have little signs round our necks saying 'Under construction', 'Refurbishment under way', 'In process of being made new – but still open for business'.

So you will find yourself dealing with *yourself* on this journey, you will get tired and want to 'opt out'. The devil will accuse you of failing again: 'See, you failed again, you're no good, you're not worth it.' But that's where we can answer back boldly that this time it's different, we're giving the mess up to God, and God has forgiven us totally.

John Newton, the converted slave-trader (who wrote the hymn 'Amazing Grace'), put it like this: 'I am not what I ought to be; but I am not what I once was. And it is by the grace of God that I am what I am.' One of the key lines in his famous hymn about the journey from salvation to heaven is: ''Tis grace hath brought me safe thus far, and grace will lead me home.' This Christian walk is a life that needs to be lived out. Don't give up. Keep pressing on

WORTH KNOWING

towards the goal – of being like Jesus and falling in love with him more and more and more.

And one day, when your journey is finally over, you'll be able to sit on the terrace of heaven – hopefully with a long, cool drink! – and look back over the winding path that was your walk there: the straight bit of path where you were determined and stomped along, the tracks that circled round and came to a dead end until you could find the way forward again, the hills and the valleys, the road where the sun shone brightly, and the awful, night-blackened dips. Then you'll be able to breathe out a long sigh and let Jesus tell you for eternity how it was truly worth it.

Ben Fogle and James Cracknell rowed the Atlantic together, finishing the 4,717-kilometre course in just under 50 days. The odds were really stacked against them on this mammoth journey and at various points their satellite phone was broken, charts lost, water desalinator bust and GPS and sea anchor gone, and they rowed day and night, getting only two hours' sleep at a time. At one point a huge storm broke over them and turned their vessel upside down. James was trapped in the cabin and Ben thrown into the enormous waves. Somehow the boat righted itself and Ben managed to swim back to climb on board, but it left both of them in a state of shock. James's wife Beverley had written him a letter, with instructions that it was only to be opened when he had reached rock bottom. James opened his letter. Among her first words to him were these: 'Just finish it, baby.'

James wept. There is something not only challenging in this statement, but incredibly tender – a sense of her trust in him to finish this race, willing him on, knowing exactly the words that would encourage him, spur him on, yet showing how much she loved him.

I believe that God is saying those words to you today. He knows you intimately and cares about you passionately. He desperately wants you to finish this 'race', this journey, this walk, and he has every hope in you to finish well. He will give you all the strength you need for whatever circumstances you are going through. And he loves you. How he loves you!

Hear his voice say to you today, 'Just finish it, baby.'

Survivor Music

Through the Valley: Lex Buckley £6.99
Lex has developed into a skilled worship leader and writer and has already contributed to the Soul Sista album Precious as well as Soul Survivor: Living Loud and We Must Go releases. Produced by Andrew Philip (Matt Redman's musical director & Soul Survivor producer) this emerge release from Lex features 8 great new songs.

Yesterday, Today & Forever Vicky Beeching £12.99
Vicky's fi rst full album displays Vicky's development into a significant worship songwriter and lead worshipper for this generation., while retaining her heart to worship. "I want to lead people into a closer and deeper revelation of God, whether they've known him for years, or are coming face to face with him for the fi rst time." Vicky Beeching

Precious: Soul Sista £6.99
7 songs written and sung by the members and supporters of Soul Sista, a ministry set up by Soul Survivor for girls only! Precious is produced by Nathan Fellingham from Phatfish and includes songs from Vicky Beeching, Lex Buckley, Beth Redman and others.

Praiseworthy: Nick Herbert £12.99
Nick Herbert is the worship pastor for St Marys Church, Marylebone, London. Through St Marys events like SOAK, Nick's songs have encouraged a generation of worshippers. There is a depth of theology that fl ows through Nick's songwriting giving songs that speak truth and fact in to worship. Contains songs co-written with Matt Redman, Tim Hughes and David Gate.

www.survivor.co.uk

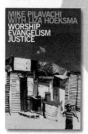

Survivor books...receive as you read

The Smile of God: Andy Hawthorne

You can t win God s favour - it s been won for you. But you can live in such a way that you know His smile on your life.

If you re tired of conforming to the pattern of the me-centred world, if you re open to the disciplines and the passions of a real man or woman of God. if you re ready to trust God in times of discouragment or outright opposition...then let this book kick start, or re you up again. God s smile awaits you.

City Changing Prayer: Debra & Frank Green

Imagine a regular city-wide gathering of Christians united and focused in prayer. Imagine a church that serves local institutions, and asks nothing in return. Imagine the crime rate falling; teenagers praying; people beginning to believe that there s something in this thing called prayer. Frank and Debra Green have seen all this and more over the past ten years. They have learnt lessons about how to foster mutual trust and spiritual fruitfulness, overcoming the obstacles both inside and outside the church family.

God on the Beach: Michael Voland

Newquay: the UK s infamous summer party capital. The town heaving with young clubbers and surfers, each one desperate to live life to the full, eager for experience, ready to ride the waves and hit the heights. Into this caotic carnival dropped Michael Volland, dj, surfer, and team member in a beach mission 21st century style. There was just one problem, Michael was not at all sure that God would turn up.

www.survivor.co.uk

Survivor books...receive as you read

Passion for Your Name: Tim Hughes

If you want to be more involved in leading worship in your church, or become a more effective member of the band, then this book is a great place to begin. Tim Hughes looks rst at the reasons why we worship God, and why we need to get our hearts right with him, before moving on to the practicalities of choosing a song list, musical dynamics, small group worship, and the art of songwriting.

Heart of Worship Files: Compiled by Matt Redman

A mixture of creative biblical insights and hands-on advice on how to lead worship and write congregational songs. Contributors include: Mike Pilavachi, Tim Hughes, Graham Kendrick, Darlene Zschech and Matt Redman. This book will encourage and inspire you to new heights of worship, giving practical advice for worship leaders, creative advice for musicians and perceptive insights into the theology of worship.

Inside Out Worship: Compiled by Matt Redman

Outside-in Worship never works, true worship always works itself from the inside, out. A love for God, which burns on the inside and cannot help to express itself externally too. Purposeful lives of worship exploding from passionate and devoted hearts. Guidance from some of today's most seasoned leaders and lead worshippers, including Darlene Zschech, Robin Mark, Tim Hughes, Chris Tomlin, Brian Houston, Terl Bryant and many more.

www.survivor.co.uk

Survivor books...receive as you read

The Lord of the Ring: Phil Anderson
In 1999, the remarkable and accidental 24-7 prayer movement began. The inspiration was a visit by founder Pete Greig to Herrnhut in Germany, when in the eighteenth century Count Zinzendorf initiated the Moravian prayer watch which ran without ceasing for a hundred years. This is Zinzendorf's story, told through the eyes of a pair of twenty-first century pilgrims seeking to rediscover it afresh. Part biography and part road-trip, it brings the history into vibrant life, while raising deeply prophetic challenges about life and faith today.

Red Moon Rising: Pete Greig
24-7 is at the centre of a prayer revival across the globe and this book gives a fantastic insight into what God is doing with ordinary prayer warriors. Read inspiring stories of people finding a new depth of heartfelt prayer and radical compassion.

The Vision & the Vow: Pete Greig
Has your faith become a chore where once it was a passion? Are you tired of the self-serving mentality of our culture? Join Pete Greig on the adventure of a lifetime in this inspiring and beautifully illustrated book; unlocking God's ultimate vision for your life and your community.

24-7 Prayer Manual
People are praying 24 hours a day, 7 days a week in countries around the world. This concise but detailed guide will help churches, youth groups, Christian Unions and groups of churches set up prayer rooms for one day, one week or one month. The book gives an introduction to the ethos of 24-7 and a step by step guide to setting up a prayer room. It's full of creative, low cost ideas that will help make the life changing prayer room experience accessible to everyone.

www.survivor.co.uk